T0094941

THE LIVES OF MAN

Also available from Quilliam Press
Classics of Muslim Spirituality

Imām ʿAbdallāh al-Ḥaddād. *The Book of Assistance,* translated by Mostafa al-Badawi (1989).

Habīb Aḥmad Mashhūr al-Ḥaddād, *Key to the Garden,* translated by Mostafa al-Badawi (1990).

Imām ʿAbdallāh al-Ḥaddād. *Gifts for the Seeker,* translated by Mostafa al-Badawi (1992).

Shaykh Abd Al-Khaliq al-Shabrawi, *Degrees of the Soul,* translated by Mostafa al-Badawi (1997).

Available from Fons Vitae

Islam in Tibet, featuring the illustrated narrative *Tibetan Caravans* by Abdul Wahid Radhu

Islam in Tibet: The Ornaments of Lhasa, video produced by Gray Henry

Suhrawardi's *Hayakal al-Nur (The Shape of Light)* interpreted by Shaykh Tosun Bayrak

Ibn ʿArabi's *Divine Governance of the Human Kingdom* interpreted by Shaykh Tosun Bayrak

Mary the Blessed Virgin of Islam by Aliah Schleifer

Motherhood in Islam by Aliah Schleifer

Shaykh al-ʿArabī ad-Darqāwī's *Letters of a Sufi Master* translated by Titus Burckhardt

Alchemy by Titus Burckhardt

THE LIVES OF MAN

A SUFI MASTER EXPLAINS THE HUMAN STATES: BEFORE LIFE, IN THE WORLD, AND AFTER DEATH

Imam ʿAbdallāh Ibn ʿAlawī Al-Ḥaddad

TRANSLATED FROM THE ARABIC BY
MOSTAFA AL-BADAWI

FONS VITAE

QUILLIAM PRESS

This edition printed and distributed by Fons Vitae, Lousiville, KY

Printed in South Korea

ISBN-1-887752-14-5

This edition published by
Fons Vitae
(Gray Henry, Director)
49 Mockingbird Valley Drive
Louisville, KY 40207-1366

website: www.fonsvitae.com

CONTENTS

EDITOR'S PREFACE

Muslims today may differ over many things, but most share a general consciousness that 'an end is near'. There is something in the air, a tense feeling of imminence, of history gathering pace for some remarkable event. This conviction is confirmed by the general unawareness of the non-Muslim collectivities, distracted by the myth of 'progress', to what is taking place. Only the Muslims, it seems, have remembered that acceleration is more usually a sign of downward than of upward motion, and that if anything is certain about it, it is that it cannot be perpetually maintained.

Hence we see that the community of Muḥammad, may blessings and peace be upon him, stands almost alone in retaining an interest in traditional, God-given, data about the end of time. The Qur'ān, as the final message given to man before the Judgement, contains very specific directions on how the last believers are to acquit themselves, and what they must expect. It is true that whole sections of the Muslim nation, engrossed by the playthings and false gods of the age, think rarely of their future existence. But most Muslims still respond vividly to Friday sermons which speak of the Last Trumpet, of the Judgement, the delights of the Garden and the torments of the Fire. In every bookshop in the Islamic world, tracts on the subject continue to outsell almost any other kind of literature, serving the Muslim desire to know the road which leads to that world which is without end.

Modern man, by contrast, trapped by an anthropology which excludes all transcendence, dehumanised by a pseudo-psychology which identifies the source of otherworldly yearning in his lowest, rather than his most exalted faculties, has been programmed to dismiss the traditional belief in an immortal soul as mythic, or even bizarre. One does not have to be a believer to know that the consequences of this new dogma have been appalling. If there is no Judgement, and hence no authentic ground of justice in the world, then morality, as secular philosophers have appreciated, is a myth. Right and wrong can at best be defined by consensus, and institutionalised by majority vote. If life is not sacred, a million unborn children can be slain in a year, and no moral law has been infringed. Further, if man's nature is not rooted in the metaphysical, if his destiny does not lie in some higher place, then his existence is desolate and meaningless, and can be articulated only through values and artforms which are broken evocations of ugliness and chaos.

No culture since Adam has lived in deeper ignorance of what man truly is: a symmetrical, noble form enshrining a soul, an organ capable of such translucence that it can, when the senses and passions which distract it are stilled, form a window onto that Reality of which this world offers no more than a distorted reflection. For those human beings who have been granted this state of awakening, the real world which they survey is truer than anything they had known here-below. All of us will see the real world, the *ākhira*, at death. But only the Prophets fully know of it before they die, and hence can warn their contemporaries. The revelations which God gives them, and which they give to mankind, are thus the only sources of meaning and understanding which will ever be available. To hold to them is to cling to a rope let down from God, while to let go is to fall ineluctably into chaos.

Muslims are aware that today's dominant culture (and we should recall that its dominance lies exclusively on the political and economic plane), is built on a single determining fact: the considered rejection of Christianity. This apostasy was the logical result of Europe's discovery that the Bible was a historical product, a distorted text in which the words of the Prophets could no longer be heard with confidence. Cut off from any reliable access to the transcendent, Europe's outlook could henceforth seek descriptions of the world only through the physical sciences, which were by definition incapable of yielding information about the *ākhira*, or about man's meaning rather than his material surroundings. Modern man thus appears as the absolute antithesis of the man of *īmān*, the man of secure awareness of the divine Reality and the tremendous destiny which awaits those who respond to it.

Although the past scholars of Islam have written innumerable works in this field, a small number have won particular popularity. These are of differing lengths and orientations: some use a rhetorical style to strike fear and hope into the heart, while others are matter-of-fact rehearsals of orthodox belief. A list of the best-known of these is offered in an appendix.

The Lives of Man is, like all the books of Imām al-Ḥaddād, remarkable for its succinctness and clarity. In this he was undoubtedly assisted by being a latecomer in Muslim history, as he was able to draw on the works of his predecessors. Like almost all ulema, he found the works of Imām al-Ghazālī to be of especial value, and this is reflected both in the content and the texture of his work.

Imām al-Ḥaddād's purpose in the *Lives* is to remind Muslims of the fact of death and the Judgement, but it is also written to help us to remind ourselves. It is not simply a list of the delights and suffering which lie beyond death, or a moralising condemnation of sin. It is far more intelligent, and far more human. Imām al-Ḥaddād was a teacher, who was visited every day by students and ordinary people from every walk of life. He knew their problems, both the outward ones and those of the soul. In particular, he knew about the *qalb* (the 'heart'), which, as the Qur'ān tells us, is an instrument of perception granted man by God: *He it is who created you, and gave you ears and eyes and hearts.* [67:23] He knew that a man might know every detail about the next life, and yet remain in a state of forgetfulness and distraction, because his *qalb* had hardened. In speaking of the Hereafter, then, the Imām chooses the material which is best calculated to awaken the heart, and fill it with the purifying fear of God, and hope for His mercy. The works of Imām al-Ḥaddād share in a trait of al-Ghazālī's writings in that one cannot read them casually. To open any page, even at random, is to have the attention caught and the heart engaged.

In these pages the reader will not find the colourful and exotic stories of the Hereafter common in many other works. There is poetry, but it is there for its effect on the soul, not because it elucidates some rare point of grammar. There is no trace of egotism or opinion. All the Imām does is to deploy the devastating Qur'ānic and authentic *ḥadīth* texts which serve the aim of his book. In short, this is Islamic scholarship at its most rigorous and effective.

Imām al-Ḥaddād begins his treatment at its logical starting point. The first 'Life of Man', he tells us, is that which we have already passed through entirely: life before conception. He cites the famous Qur'ānic verse (7:172) which describes how the souls of all mankind were taken forth from Adam's loins, and made to declare their faith in the divine unity. The memory of this, preserved in the embryonic human consciousness, fades before birth.

The Second Life is our existence in the *dunyā*, that tiny slice of reality with which we are most familiar. Imām al-Ḥaddād explains that life in this period divides into five stages: childhood, youth, maturity, seniority and decrepitude, and that man has distinct spiritual requirements and abilities in each of these.

The Third Life begins at the moment of death, when man enters the *Barzakh*, literally, the 'intermediate realm' which separates the *dunyā* from the events of the Judgement. All people are visited by two angels, Munkar and Nakīr, to be asked about their beliefs and their actions, after which they receive a foretaste of their future experiences in the Garden or the Fire. The chapter includes a discussion on how the living may help the dead, and examines the question of visiting graves and tombs. It closes with a brief treatment of the coming of Jesus and Imām Mahdī (upon them be peace), and the Dajjāl.

The Fourth Life takes the reader through the events of the Judgement: the Trumpet-Blast, the Gathering, the Bridge, the Balance, and the Intercession (*shafāʿa*) of the Messenger, may blessings and peace be upon him.

The book then moves on to the everlasting Fifth Life, describing the uproar of the Fire, and the crystalline, archetypal perfection of Paradise. Following the example of Imām Ghazālī, it closes on an optimistic note, with a short Afterword on the Vision (*ru'ya*) of God's Face, which will be granted to the blessed in Heaven, together with a sequence of *ḥadīths* describing God's ultimate mercy and compassion for His creatures.

We ask God the Exalted to render us among those He takes from life in the best of states, and protects from the trials of the life which is to come. Āmīn.

ABDAL-HAKIM MURAD

London 1411

FOREWORD

In the name of God, the Merciful and Compassionate.

Praise is for God, Maker of the heavens and the earth, Creator of all beings. And may blessings and peace rest upon our master Muḥammad, the most noble of His creatures, who was sent with truth and guidance as a mercy to the worlds, and upon his Family and Companions, the good and perfect ones, and those who follow them with goodness until the Day of Judgement.

One of the best things I have ever come across and been guided to, among the treasures left by Shaykh al-Islām, Ḥujjat al-Anām, Imām ʿAbdallāh ibn ʿAlawī al-Ḥaddād, al-ʿAlawī al-Ḥaḍramī al-Shāfiʿī (may God grant benefit by him), is this rare and precious treatise known as *The Lives of Man*, which embodies a statement of the situations and stages through which man must pass, namely:

1. His passage down from the beginning through the loins of his male and female ancestors before his birth.
2. The period of his life, from his birth to his death.
3. The period spent in the Intermediate Realm after his death, until the Day of Resurrection.
4. The period spent at the Gathering-Place after the Resurrection, and until final judgement is passed.
5. Life in the Abode of Permanence, whether in the delight of the Gardens or the flames of the Fire.

In each of these 'lives', Imām al-Ḥaddād provides a full exposition of the stages and events which man must expect, basing his words on the revealed texts, in a way which is straightforward, clear, and refreshes the soul. The reader finds himself illuminated, and guided to truth and certitude, and is protected thereby from slipping into the shadows of misguidance. Each 'Life' is followed by an important 'Afterword' based on its message.

Muslims, especially in our time, direly need to learn everything about these realities, and to make a complete study of the details involved, in order to know about the stages of human life—especially the stage during which we are accountable under the *Sharīʿa*, and the consequences of obedience and rebellion, namely reward and chastisement, profit and loss, in this world and the next. As a result, the intelligent reader will be enabled to tread the best path, until he attains to felicity in both worlds. And it is those who enjoy God's guidance who shall be blessed with success.

Ḥasanayn Muḥammad Makhlūf

Formerly Grand Mufti of Egypt
Member of the Senior Ulema Council

THE WAY TO REMEMBER AND LEARN FROM THE LIVES OF MAN THAT WANE AND PERISH

Prologue

In the Name of God, the Merciful and Compassionate.
Lord give us ease, You are Generous!
Transcendent are You! We have no knowledge save that which You have taught us. You are indeed the Knowing, the Wise! [2:32]

ALL PRAISE BELONGS TO GOD, the One, the Overpowering, the Eminent, the Forgiving, the Manager of all affairs, the Maker of destinies, Who makes day pass into night and night pass into day, as a lesson and a reminder to people endowed with eyesight and understanding.

Transcendent, High, and Holy is the Formidable King, the Proud Compeller; He is Ancient and Pre-Existent, Permanent and Eternal, Alive and Self-Subsistent; Who has ordained that His creatures be subject to extinction and passing-away, to death and decay, to change from state to state, and motion from abode to abode. He alone has permanence across all the ages, stages and lifetimes that wane and perish. I praise Him as He has praised Himself and as do His sincere good servants, the Angels Brought Nigh, the Prophets who are sent, and righteous, foremost servants.

Blessings and peace be upon His slave and Messenger, our master and patron Muḥammad, the chosen and designated one, who was sent as a *Mercy to the Worlds*, and a Seal to the

Prophets, and upon the pure and good People of his House, his Companions, both Emigrants and Helpers, and those who follow them with excellence until the Day of Judgement and Reward, when mankind shall be separated into two groups, one for the Garden and one for the Fire.

This is, God willing, a blessed book, written for the purpose of remembering and assimilating the lessons contained in the different lives and states through which a human being passes, beginning with his movement from the loin to the womb, until he finds his halting-place either in the Garden or the Fire.

God exhorted His messenger, may blessings and peace be upon him, to remind mankind, and has made reminding one of the hallmarks of the believers, the people of repentance, apprehension, hearts, and attentiveness. For He has said: *Remind, for reminding profits believers.* [51:55] *Therefore remind, for by the grace of your Lord you are neither a soothsayer nor a madman.* [52:29] *Therefore remind, for the reminder yields benefit. He will heed who fears.* [87:9–10] *Remind them, for you are but a remembrancer, not a ruler over them.* [88:21–2] *None pays heed save him who turns [unto Him] repentant.* [40:13] *Indeed in this is a reminder for him who has a heart, or gives ear with attentiveness.* [50:37]

It has been related that when God the Exalted revealed: *So withdraw from them, for you are in no wise to blame,* [52:54] the Messenger of God, may blessings and peace be upon him, felt greatly sad, fearing that their punishment had become imminent and that no hope of their accepting his guidance remained. So God revealed to him: *Remind, for reminding profits believers,* [51:55] and he was happy and relieved. For God had made his nature to be one of mercy and compassion for all, eager to counsel and attract them to truth and guidance. God had sent him to them as a mercy, describing him thus in His Book: *There has come to you a Messenger, [one] of yourselves; grievous to him is your suffering, full of concern for you, for the believers gentle and compassionate.* [9:128] And since this was his nature, he was distressed by their refusal to accept truth and guidance, as God the Exalted said: *Yet it may be, if they believe not in these words, that you will torment yourself, after them, with grief.* [18:6]

A 'life' ['*umr*] is a 'period of time', as can be understood from His saying (Exalted is He!): *Say: If God had so willed, I would not have recited it to you, nor would He have made it known to you. I dwelt among you a lifetime before it; do you not understand?* [10:16] meaning the forty years from his birth (peace be upon him) to the time when God made him a Messenger among his people in Mecca the Ennobled.

We have felt it good to divide the lengthy duration of man[1] into five 'lives', even though there are different stages and states within each of these lives. But although man goes through a whole range of developments, some of which he is aware of, and some not (as He has said (Exalted is He!): *We will make you grow again into what you do not know* [56:61]), nonetheless, his essence remains his essence, and he is not other than himself, throughout this gamut of changes and stages, and he is aware of himself and whatever good or evil, reward or punishment, comes to him.

The thought of writing this treatise occurred to me a long time ago, but I resolved to postpone it until I had passed sixty-three years of age, which was, according to the most authentic sources, the lifespan of the Messenger of God, may blessings and peace be upon him. (Others have said that he was sixty, while still others say sixty-five.) This number of years has now elapsed, and I am now several months into my sixty-seventh year. I ask God for the good of it, and for its *baraka*, and a good ending, and ask His protection against its evils, temptations and a bad ending; He is the Best to be asked and the Most Generous in whom is our hope. We ask and implore Him to 'let us live so long as life is better for us, and die when death is better for us'. O Lord God! Do not hasten with us to punishment, nor delay us until we be tempted! O Lord God! We ask of You the good of life, the good of death, and the good that lies in between! And we seek Your protection against the evil in life, the evil in death, and the evil that lies in between! O Lord God! Give us the life of the blessed, those whom You wish to make endure, and give us the death of the martyrs, those whom You love to meet! Make our ending and that of those whom we loved and are loved by, our friends in You, and all Muslims, be in goodness and excellence, in gentleness and wellbeing, O Most Merciful of the Merciful! Āmīn.

The title of this treatise is *The Way to Remember and Learn from the Lives of Man that Wane and Perish.* We ask God to make its benefit widespread, to make its intention be purely for the sake of His noble Face, and for drawing closer to His Good Pleasure and to being with Him in the Gardens of Felicity, through His grace, mercy, generosity and magnanimity, for He is the Magnanimous, the Generous, the Good and the Merciful.

It is now time to start with the book we have intended. It is the True God Who gives help and makes matters easy; He guides to truth. *My success is only by God, on Him do I depend, to Him do I return.* [11:88] *He is my Lord, there is no God but Him, on Him do I depend, and unto Him do I repent.* [13:30]

Know that we have investigated the number of lives through which the children of Adam pass, and have found it possible to reduce them to five, each of which encloses stages and states within itself. People differ from each other in some of these, and resemble each other in others.

The first life began when God created Adam, upon whom be peace, and set in his loins all his descendants, the happy among them, and the wretched.[2] Then each person is continually passed on from loin to womb, and from womb to loin, until he comes out from between his father and his mother.

The second life is from the time when a man comes out into the world until the time when he dies and departs from it.

The third life extends from the time he leaves the world

through death until the time he is resurrected following the Blast on the Horn. This is the 'intermediate realm' [*barzakh*].

The fourth life begins when he emerges from his grave—or wherever else God may will him to be—at the Blast on the Horn for the Day of Resurrection and Rising, to be assembled and stand before God, to endure the Balance [*Mīzān*] and the Reckoning, then the passage over the Bridge [*Ṣirāṭ*] and the receiving of his scroll, together with all the other circumstances, hardships, and terrors of the Day of Rising.

The fifth life begins when he enters the Garden eternally, which is the age which is inexhaustible and without limit. It also begins for the people of the Fire when they enter it, after which their conditions are to differ: some will remain there endlessly and eternally, namely the unbelievers [*kāfirūn*] of whichever kind, while others will be permitted to leave it, who are the sinful among the people of *tawḥīd*, and who will leave it either through intercession [*shafāʿa*] or by some other way which we shall write on at greater length when we come to expand on the fifth life.

We will, however, keep our commentary on each of those lives brief, as befits the time and the circumstances, avoiding excessive detail but with enough information to achieve the purpose properly and to explain those issues about which people often ask. A fully detailed exposition would be impossible, as it would need very lengthy explanations and tedious elaborations.

THE FIRST LIFE

Life Before Conception

The first life begins with God's creation of Adam, upon whom be peace, and the entrusting of his progeniture [*dhurrīya*] to his blessed loins, both the people of the Right and those of the Left, namely the people of the Two Fistfuls.[3]

Then God brought this progeniture out from Adam's loins all at once, to take the covenant [*mīthāq*] that they recognised [His] Unity and Lordship. This event, which happened at Nuʿmān, a valley near ʿArafāt, is referred to in His saying (Exalted is He!): *When your Lord brought forth from the Children of Adam, from their loins, their seed, and made them testify of themselves* [*He said:*] *'Am I not your Lord?' They said, 'Yea! We testify!'* [*That was*] *lest you should say on the Day of Rising: 'Of this we were unaware'.* [7:172] The verse following this refers to it also.[4] It has been related in Tradition that when He took the Covenant, He recorded it in writing and fed it to the Black Stone, and that this was the meaning of the saying of those who touch the Black Stone during the circumambulation of the Ancient House: 'O God! This is believing in You, fulfilling our pledge to You, and declaring the truth of Your Record!'

Because of these things, there can be no doubt that the progeniture was possessed of existence, hearing, and speech; this, however, was at a degree or dimension of existence other than that of this world. There are many levels of existence, as is well known by those people who know existence.

It is narrated that the Messenger of God, may blessings and

peace be upon him, was already a Prophet when Adam was between water and clay, between spirit and body, and that he accompanied Adam when he was brought down [from the Garden], Noah when he boarded the Ark, and Abraham when he was thrown into Nimrod's fire. Although this applies to all the progeniture carried in the loins of the Prophets mentioned here—upon them be peace—the existence of the Messenger of God, may blessings and peace be upon him, at this stage was more perfect and complete. Perhaps this consisted of a knowledge and awareness of what was happening which remained with him until he appeared in the world [*dunyā*]. This saying of his was to distinguish him from others by virtue of that which was specific to him alone. As for the rest of the progeniture, it is possible that they had some kind of awareness during those conditions, especially at the time when they pledged their covenant, but neither the awareness nor the knowledge persisted with them as it did with him—may blessings and peace be upon him.

The progeniture was undoubtedly in Adam's loins even in the Garden, as is evidenced by the *ḥadīth* of the Intercession: 'Did He expel you from the Garden, save for the sin of your father Adam?' and the debate between Moses and Adam, upon both of whom be peace: 'You are the one who caused the people to be expelled from the Garden through your sin!'[5]

It has been related that when God took them all out of Adam's loins, the Angels saw that they had filled all the plains and all the rough places, and they said: 'O Lord! The world will not suffice them.' But He said: 'I am creating Death.' At this they said: 'Then they will never be happy in life,' and He said: 'I am creating hope.'

And it is related that when God took Adam's progeniture out from his loins, Adam saw one individual amongst them who was particularly handsome, so he asked who he was, to be told: 'He is your son David, upon whom be peace.' And Adam asked his Lord: 'How long did You make his lifespan?' The Exalted replied: 'Sixty years.' Adam asked for his life to be increased, and was told that that was what He had written for him, so he said: 'I wish to give him forty years out of my own life.' And God had already written a thousand years to be Adam's life. The *ḥadīth* is very well known.

And when Moses, upon whom be peace, saw in the Torah[6] the description of a praiseworthy nation [*umma*] possessed of noble attributes, he asked who they were and who their Prophet might be, and entreated God to make them be his own nation. He was told: 'They are the nation of Aḥmad.' He then asked God to show this nation to him, and God made it appear before him. We will probably quote this *ḥadīth* in full at the end of [our writing on] this Life. It is quoted in some Qur'ānic commentaries in the context of His saying: *And you were not beside the Mountain when We called.* [28:46]

It is evident from what we have mentioned, and other things which we have not, that the progeniture had, prior to their appearance in the world, an existence appropriate to their [degree of] knowledge, and that the Messenger of God, may blessings and peace be upon him, had a more perfect, complete, and significant one. This was referred to by al-ʿAbbās, the uncle of God's Messenger, may God bless him and grant him peace, in some verses of poetry in which he praised the Prophet:

> Anciently you were good in the shadows,
> and in a storeplace, when the [fig]leaf was attached
> Then you came down to the land, not as a man,
> nor a lump of foetal flesh, nor a bloodclot.
> Rather, a seed which rode the ark,
> having shattered Nasr, its people submerged.
> You were brought from loin to womb;
> when a world passed, another appeared.
> Until your guardian House contained
> an exalted Khandaf guarded by veils.

Nasr was one of the idols of Noah's people, while Khandaf was the wife of Ilyās ibn Muḍar, and hence an ancestor of God's Messenger, may God bless him and grant him peace.

It is narrated that Adam, upon whom be peace, used to hear the light of the Messenger of God, may blessings and peace be upon him, glorifying [God] within his loins, making a rustling sound like that of birds, until Eve became pregnant with Seth, may peace be on them both; so it was transmitted to her, then to Seth, upon whom be peace, then from pure loins to radiant wombs until the Messenger of God, may blessings and peace be upon him, appeared between his noble parents, untouched by any of the uncleanness or dirt of the Age of Ignorance [*jāhilīya*]. In those days some invalid forms of marriage were being practiced, but God kept him pure from such things, and he said, may blessings and peace be upon him: 'I came forth from wedlock, not from unchastity.'

Ibn ʿAbbās, may God be pleased with him, commented on the verses: *The One Who sees you when you stand up [in prayer], and when you turn about in those who prostrate* [26:218–9] by saying that this referred to his transmission, may blessings and peace be upon him, from Prophet's loin to Prophet's loin; for [Prophets in his ancestry include] Ishmael, Abraham, Noah, Seth, and Adam—peace be upon them all. There is no disagreement [among scholars] on this.

As for his meeting with Adam in the Terrestrial Heaven [*samā' al-dunyā*], this was during the *Miʿrāj*, during his life of the world and while Adam was in the Intermediate Realm.

As for that blackness that he saw to the right and the left of Adam, upon whom be peace, and was told when asked about it that it consisted of the souls of his children, it is possible that they were those of them who had died and whose distinguishing deeds had appeared—although there are other possibilities.

And finally, the meeting of Moses with Adam, peace be upon them both, when the debate between them occurred, may have been when they were both in the Intermediate Realm. There are also other possibilities, and only God knows best what the reality of this was.

Afterword

To conclude this life, we will quote in full, as promised, the *ḥadīth* which gives the description of the Muḥammadan nation.

Wahb ibn Munabbih, may God show him His mercy, said: 'When Moses, upon whom be peace, read the Tablets, he found mentioned in them the merits of the nation of Muḥammad, may blessings and peace be upon him, and he said: "O Lord! Which is this mercy-given nation that I find in the Tablets?" God answered: "It is the nation of Aḥmad, whose people are content with whatever little provision I give them, and I am content with whatever little good works they do. I make each one of them enter the Garden by his testimony that *Lā ilāha illa'Llāh*".

'And then Moses said: "I find in the Tablets a nation of people who shall be resurrected and assembled on the Day of Rising with their faces like full moons. Let them be my nation!" But God replied: "They are the nation of Aḥmad; I shall gather them resurrected on the Day of Rising, when their foreheads and limbs shall be blazing white from the effect of their *wuḍū'*-ablutions and their prostrations."

'Moses said: "O Lord! I find in the Tablets a nation of people whose clothes are on their backs[7] and whose swords are on their shoulders, people of certitude and dependence [*tawakkul*]; they glorify God from minaret-tops, and they continue to seek to fight for every righteous cause, until they do battle against the Dajjāl. Let them be my nation!" But He said: "They are the nation of Aḥmad!"

'Moses said: "O Lord! I find in the Tablets a nation of people who pray five times each day and night, at five hours of the day, for whom the gates of Heaven are opened and upon whom mercy descends; let them be my nation!" But He replied: "They are the nation of Aḥmad."

'Moses said: "O Lord! I find in the Tablets a nation for whom the [whole] earth is a place of worship and ritually pure, and for whom booty is lawful; let them be my nation!" But He replied: "They are the nation of Aḥmad."

'Moses said: "O Lord! I find in the Tablets a nation of people who fast the month of Ramaḍān for You, and whom You then forgive all they had done before; let them be my nation!" But He replied: "They are the nation of Aḥmad."

'Moses said: "O Lord! I find in the Tablets a nation of people who go on pilgrimage to the Inviolable House for Your sake, whose longing for it is never exhausted, whose weeping is loud and tumultuous, whose *talbiya* is clamorous; let them be my nation!" But He said: "They are the nation of Aḥmad."

'Moses said: "What will You give them for that?" And God said: "I shall grant them more forgiveness, and shall allow them to intercede for those who come after them."

'Moses said: "O Lord! I find in the Tablets a nation of people who ask forgiveness for their sins; when they raise their food to their mouths it does not reach their stomachs before they are forgiven; they start [eating] with Your Name and end with Your praise; let them be my nation!" But He said: "They are the nation of Aḥmad."

'Moses said: "O Lord! I find in the Tablets a nation whose members will be the foremost on the Day of Rising, but are the last to be created; let them be my nation!" But He replied: "They are the nation of Aḥmad."

'Moses said: "O Lord! I find in the Tablets a nation of people whose gospels are held within their breasts and they recite them; let them be my nation!" But He answered: "They are the nation of Aḥmad."

'Moses said: "O Lord! I find in the Tablets a nation of people among whom, when one of them intends a good deed but does not perform it, it is written as one good deed for him, while if he does perform it, it is written as ten to seven hundred times its worth; let them be my nation!" But God said: "They are the nation of Aḥmad."

'Moses said: "O Lord! I find in the Tablets a nation among whom, when one of them intends a sin but does not commit it, it is not recorded against him, while if he does commit it, it is written as a single sin; let them be my nation!" But He replied: "They are the nation of Aḥmad."

'Moses said: "O Lord! I find in the Tablets a nation who are the best of people, who *exhort to good and forbid evil*; let them be my nation!" But He said: "They are the nation of Aḥmad."

'Moses said: "O Lord! I find in the Tablets a nation of people who will be resurrected and brought on the Day of Rising as three groups. One group shall enter the Garden without *reckoning, another's reckoning will be easy*, and another will be rigorously judged, then made to enter the Garden; let them be my nation!" But He said: "They are the nation of Aḥmad."

'Moses said: "O Lord! You have spread out all this goodness for Aḥmad and his nation; let me be a member of his nation!" But God told him: "O Moses! I have chosen and preferred you over other people with My Message and My Speech; take what I have given you, and be one of the thankful."'

Ibn ʿAbbās, God be pleased with him, said: 'The Messenger of God, may blessings and peace be upon him, said one day to his Companions: "What do you say of this verse: *And you were not beside the Mountain when We called?*" [28:46] They said: "God and His Messenger know best." And he told them, "When God spoke to Moses, upon whom be peace, he asked Him: 'O Lord! Have You created any creature dearer to You than myself? For You have chosen and preferred me over mankind, and did speak to me on Mount Sinai.' And God answered him, saying: 'O Moses! Did you not know that Muḥammad is dearer to me than the rest of My creation? And that I looked into the hearts of My slaves, and, finding no heart humbler than yours, therefore chose and preferred you, with My Message and My Speech, over other men. Make sure, therefore, that you die in *Tawḥīd* and the love of Muhammad!'

'Moses asked again: 'O Lord! Is there any nation dearer to you than mine? For You have *shaded* them with *the cloud, and sent down to them honeydew* [manna] *and quails.'* [2:57] And God replied: 'O Moses! Did you not know that the eminence of the nation of Muḥammad over other nations is like My eminence over the whole of My creation?' Moses asked: 'O Lord! Will I see them?' And He replied: 'You will not see them, but if you wish, you can hear their speech.' Moses said: 'I do so wish.' And thus God the Exalted called: 'O nation of Muḥammad!' And they all answered with one voice, from within the loins of their ancestors: '*Labbayk Allāhumma, Labbayk*! [Here we are, O God! Here we are!]'. And God the Exalted said: 'My blessings and peace are upon you; My Mercy has outstripped My Wrath; My Forgiveness has outstripped My Punishment; I forgave you before you even asked for My Forgiveness; I answered you before you called upon Me; I gave to you before you asked of Me! Those of you who will meet me bearing witness that there is no god save God and that Muḥammad is the Messenger of God, I will forgive them their sins.'"

'And the Prophet, upon whom be blessings and peace, continued, and said: "And God wished to favour me with this, so He said (Exalted is He!): *And you were not beside the Mountain when We called*; i.e. [when We called] your nation to let Moses hear them speak."'[8]

THE SECOND LIFE

"Dunyā" – *the Lower World*

The second life begins when one is delivered from one's mother's womb, and ends when one departs from the world in death. This, which is the middle of the lives, is also their purpose. It is the period when man is held accountable for [responding to] the divine injunctions and prohibitions, the consequences of which will be reward or punishment, endless happiness in the proximity of God, the High and Majestic, or perpetual torment and remoteness from Him.

Great individual differences exist between people as regards the length or brevity of this period, as also in other respects.

In the Womb

This life begins with a prologue which resembles the Intermediary World of the life-to-come, in which there appear many of those factors which cause one person to take precedence over another after the resurrection, and where some of the essences of worldly matters which pertained to the person before his death are retained. This 'prologue' is the period of gestation, for it sees the appearance of some of the wordly influences which will apply to a person after his leaving his mother's womb, just as he retains something of the essences of the special existence within loins and wombs in which he had lived before he appeared in his mother's womb. God mentions gestation, these phenomena, and the stages through which it passes in many verses in His eminent Book:

> *We created man from a product of clay. Then We placed him as a drop in a safe lodging, then We made of the lump bones, then We covered the bones with flesh, and then brought him forth as another creation. So blessed be God, the Best of Creators!* [23:12–4]

> *O Mankind! Should you be in doubt concerning the Resurrection, then [know that] We created you from dust, then from a drop of seed, then from a clot, then from a lump of flesh shapely and shapeless, that We may make it clear for you. And We cause what We will to remain in the wombs for an appointed time.* [22:5]

There are also many *Ḥadīths* on this subject, one of the most comprehensive being that of ʿAbdallāh ibn Masʿūd, may God be pleased with him, as recorded by Bukhārī and Muslim:

> The Messenger of God, upon whom be blessings and peace, told us—and he is the Truthful whose veracity God confirms—'Any one of you will have had his created existence brought together in his mother's womb, as a drop [*nuṭfa*] for forty days, then a sticky attached clot [*ʿalaqa*] for the same [period], then a piece of flesh [*muḍgha*] for the same period, after which God sends the angel to blow the spirit [*rūḥ*] into him. The angel is commanded to write four words: his [apportioned] provision, his lifespan, his deeds, and whether he will end up as wretched or joyful. By the One besides Whom there is no other god! One of you may do the works of the people of the Garden, until he is [separated from it] only by an arm's length, then that which had been written overtakes him and he does the works of the people of the Fire, and enters it. And one of you may do the works of the people of the Fire until nothing remains

> between him and it but an arm's length; then that which had been written overtakes him, he does the works of the people of the Garden, and so enters it.'

This authentic *Ḥadīth* contains enough to put great fear into the obedient and righteous, let alone the rebellious and the sinners.

Childhood

Man thus remains in his mother's belly until God wills him to come forth. This is the first part of his life in this world [*dunyā*]. God the Exalted has mentioned the beginning of this Life in His Book, stating how man moves from stage to stage, and from one condition to the next:

> *And afterward We bring you forth as infants, then [give you growth] that you attain your full strength. And among you are those who die, and others who are brought back to the worst time of life, so that after having had knowledge they know nothing at all.* [22:5]

> *Then that you attain full strength, and then that you became old—though some among you die before—and that you reach an appointed term, that you may perhaps understand.* [40:67]

And there are many more verses relating to this.

In this second Life people move from the state of childhood to puberty, then to youth, to young adulthood, to maturity and seniority, and then to such decrepitude and senility as God may will, all in accordance with what God has said in His Book.

When a human being is born he begins to scream, which is due to his being stabbed by Satan (may God curse him). Only Jesus son of Mary, and his mother, upon them be peace, escaped this; for God guarded them against it because of the prayers of Mary's mother ('Imrān's wife): *"I seek Your protection for her and for her offspring from Satan the repudiate".* [3:36] This also finds mention in a *ḥadīth*: Iblīs arrived to stab but his thrust came against the [protective] veil.

It is a *sunna*, which we are commanded to follow, to give the call to prayer [*Adhān*] in the right ear of a newborn baby, and the *Iqāma* in its left ear, to remind the child of its primordial nature [*fiṭra*] according to which God has made people, namely *Tawḥīd*. The Messenger of God, upon whom be blessings and peace, said: 'Every newborn baby has, when born, his *fiṭra*; it is his parents who make of him a Jew, a Christian, or a Zoroastrian.' And God the Exalted said: *So set your face to the religion, as a man by nature upright, the nature [fiṭra] [given by] God in which He has created mankind.* [30:30]

It is an absolutely duty for both parents to protect their child from everything that might distort his *fiṭra*, to raise him well, protect him from evil nurses, and seriously strive to do these things, for as a *ḥadīth* says, suckling alters nature. In his heart they must plant a reverence for the symbols of religion and for the things God has made sacrosanct, the love of goodness, the practice of it, and of its practitioners. They must encourage and exhort him to do good, and discourage him from and make hateful to him evil, the practice of it, and those who practice it. They must also uproot love for the world and its pleasures from his heart, together with the inclination to enjoy it, and they must neither assist him in enjoying the *dunyā* nor render it easy for him, for that would be harming him, and would cause him to diverge from the straight Way.

They must tell him to pray when he reaches seven years of age, and to fast as much as he can manage. From the age of ten onwards they are to discipline him physically should he neglect these duties. They should prevent him from associating with bad company, and people whose dominant state is heedlessness and frivolousness, whether they be young or old. They must take even greater care with him as he develops the signs of discernment, and not allow him to say or do anything which is not pleasant and praiseworthy, so that he grows up in this manner, as these things become a firmly established habit in him, which will make it easy for him to practice them when grown up, for goodness is a habit. Most of the duties connected to this must be performed by parents and other guardians. It is also important to keep the child away from children of people of no goodness or of bad families, for it has been said that 'the ruining of children stems mostly from other children'. In the volume on disciplining the soul in the *Iḥyā'*, the Imām, the Proof of Islam, may God have mercy on him, has written comprehensively about how to discipline children and bring them up well.[9]

This period, from birth to puberty, is one in which God has lightened the load. For children are not obliged to pray, fast, or perform any other obligation of the *Sharīʿa*, save what their guardians exhort them to do. 'The pen is withheld from [recording the deeds of] three people: a child until he reaches puberty, a sleeper until he awakes, and a madman until he recovers.' [*Ḥadīth.*] Such is the graciousness, generosity and gentleness of God. Any act of religious observance that a child does before puberty is recorded in his Muslim parents' scrolls. To the extent that they bring him up well and as they should, it is to be hoped that, through God's grace, they will not be deprived of the reward for his acts of goodness and religious observance after he has reached puberty, but that they will each receive as much reward for them as he does. This is borne out by the *ḥadīth* where inviting to guidance and guiding to goodness are mentioned, for this is what they will have done.[10]

When the child reaches puberty—assuming that he is sane — he becomes accountable [*mukallaf*], and God's discourse becomes addressed to him, including His injunctions and prohibitions, promises and warnings, rewards and punishments, and God commands the two Noble Guardian Angels to record his good and evil deeds, the one on the right his good deeds, the one on the left his sins. God the Exalted says:

Indeed, above you are guardians, noble and recording, aware of what you do. [82:11–2] *When the two Receivers receive* [*him*], *seated on the right and on the left, he utters no word but there is with him an observer, ready.* [50:17–8]

They are commanded to scrutinise and remember all that he says or does, whether good or evil, throughout his life and until his death, after which they appear with him on the Day of Rising when he comes to stand before God, and they bear witness for or against him. *And every soul comes; with it is a driver and witness.* [50:21]

When the child reaches puberty, his[1] father or guardian should remind him anew of the articles of faith, and the obligations and prohibitions, even if he has already been taught these things, for he has now entered upon a new stage, and his situation is different. Even though at puberty he has become accountable [for himself], he still needs encouragement, reminding, and explanations about what he has become accountable for: about religious obligations such as prayers and fasting, and keeping away from prohibited things such as adultery, homosexuality, alcohol-drinking, and wrongfully consuming other people's money whether by usury, coercion, deceit, or any other method. Although these are things any sane adult should seek to understand himself, if he has not been informed about them prior to reaching adulthood, it remains the duty of his parents and guardians to encourage and prompt him both to learn and to practice what he learns. This constitutes either an obligation [*wājib*] or a firm recommendation [*mandūb muta'akkid*], depending on the condition both of the parents and of their offspring.

Youth

After the onset of puberty, the first stage of youth begins, a stage where energy is abundant and strength is continually increasing, which means that it is the stage most suited for winning rewards, doing good works, and avoiding sins and reprehensible acts. However it is also a hazardous stage of which one should be wary, for many or even most young people are inclined toward worldly desires, and prefer immediate pleasures to decent actions and observances.

It is unusual to find a youth established in obedience, longing for good works, and neglectful of worldly desires and ephemeral pleasures. 'Your Lord wonders at a young man who shows no passions.' [*Ḥadīth.*] And the Messenger of God, may blessings and peace be upon him, included among the seven that God will shade with His shade 'on the day when no shade shall exist save His', a 'young man who grew up in the service of God'. It has been related that God the Exalted said: 'O young man, who has abandoned his passions for My sake: you are to Me as are some of My angels.'

Hence young people should be very careful to protect themselves against being dragged into God's wrath and painful chastisement simply by their youthfulness; let them instead make it into a means and ladder leading up to the good-pleasure of God and His tremendous reward. Let them remember the advice of God's Messenger, upon whom be blessings and peace, for he has more compassion and solicitude for us than ourselves, our fathers, and our mothers. He said: 'Seize [the opportunity to make use of] five [things] before five [other things catch up with you]: your youth before you grow old, your health before you fall sick, your leisure before you are occupied, your wealth before you grow poor, and your life before you die.' And he said, upon him be blessings and peace: 'The feet of a servant will not move away [from where he stands on the Day of Rising] until he is asked about five things: his life, and how he expended it, his youth, and in what he exhausted it, his wealth, and where he obtained it and on what he spent it,' etc.

Youth is the time when acquiring merit, knowledge, and attaining to positions of religious leadership and eminence are possible. One poet has said:

> If a youth has nothing to boast of when he reaches
> twenty years, he'll never have anything to boast of.

Another declared:

> If you do not prevail in the nights of youth,
> then you shall never prevail, though you live long.
> Is most of your life other than youth?
> Take what you can from it, and neglect it not.

Those of our righteous predecessors who lived long in the way of God and in His obedience used to urge young people to seize the chance offered by their youth, saying: 'Use your youth before you became like us: old, feeble and too weak to perform many acts of goodness.' They said this even though despite their circumstances they were outstripping youngsters in striving for God, and in zeal and determination in His obedience.

Maturity

A young person then moves on to the 'Age of Maturity', which sees the peak of one's lifetime and the attainment of one's full power.

Ibn al-Jawzī divides the human lifespan into five periods. The first, childhood, ends at the age of fifteen; the second, youth, extends to the age of thirty-five; the third, maturity, ends at the age of fifty; the fourth, seniority, ends at the age of seventy; while the fifth, that of decrepitude, must terminate in death. Other scholars provide more or less similar divisions.

At the peak of one's faculties and maturity one may expect to attain wisdom, which God gives to those fit to receive it. Repentance and the return to God predominate for the fortunate bondsman who has God's caring eye upon him. God the Exalted has said: *And when he attained his prime, We gave him wisdom and strength, and thus do We reward the good,* [12:22] and: *Until when he attained full strength and reached forty years, he said: 'My Lord: Inspire me to give thanks for that with which You have favoured me, and my parents, and to do the good works that are pleasing to You. And be gracious to me in the matter of my seed. Truly, I have turned unto You repentant, and truly, I am of those who are Muslims'.* [46:15]

At the age of forty the Messenger of God, upon whom be blessings and peace, received the revelation from God and became an envoy to all mankind, *a bearer of good tidings and of warning.*[11]

It almost becomes clear at this Age whether any particular person is ultimately intended for good or evil, virtue or corruption, for there are certain signs which appear and predominate, to the extent that if – as some have said – a man has attained the age of forty and the goodness in him has not become dominant over his evil, the Devil rubs his face and cries: 'A face that will never succeed!' It is also said that whoever reaches forty without the goodness in him having become dominant over his evil, should prepare himself for the Fire. Some scholars have said that the age of forty is that age referred to by God the Exalted in His words: *Did We not grant you a life long enough for him who reflects to reflect therein? And the warner came to you.* [35:37] Others have said that it is the age of sixty—and this is the more authentic view.

The gnostic Shaykh ʿAbdal-Wahhāb ibn Aḥmad al-Shaʿrānī writes in *al-Baḥr al-Mawrūd*:

> Our oaths were taken that when we reached forty years of age we would fold up our sleeping mats except when overpowered [by sleep], and remain constantly aware with each breath that we are travellers to the Hereafter, so that no rest remains to us in the world; we must see each atom of our life past forty as equal to a hundred years prior to that; there must be no repose for us, no competition over positions, no joy over anything worldly. All this is

> because life is narrowed after forty, and heedlessness, distraction and playing are inappropriate for him who nears the battleground of deaths.

Imām Mālik used to say: 'We used to know people who studied until they were forty, after which they would so occupy themselves with practising what they knew that they had no free time left to turn to anything worldly.'

And when Imām al-Shāfiʿī, may God show him His mercy, reached forty he began to walk with a staff, and when questioned about it used to say: 'To remind myself that I am a traveller.'

By God! I now see myself like a caged bird who extricated himself until only his heel remained caught up in the cage. Since this is now my condition, I have no residual desire to remain in the world; and I grant no permission to any of my companions to give me anything of the world or mention any of its affairs, except that which is legally necessary to me. I say: '*God is my sufficiency*! May God make all brethren thus! Amīn!'

Wahb ibn Munabbih, may God show him His mercy, said: 'I have read somewhere that each morning a herald announces from the fourth heaven: "O people of forty! You are a crop whose harvest is nigh! O people of fifty! What have you sent ahead of you, and what have you kept back? O –people of sixty! You have no excuse! Would that creatures had never been created! When created, they know why they are created. The Hour has come to you, so beware!"'

Seniority

Then man moves on from manhood to 'seniority' [*shaykhūkha*] which according to Ibn al-Jawzī extends from fifty to seventy. God the Exalted has said: *Then He brings you forth as a child, then that you attain your full strength, and afterward that you become old people, though some of you die before, and that you reach an appointed term, that you may understand.* [40:67]

At this time the earliest signs of weakness begin to appear, strength recedes, and the period from sixty to seventy is that which the Messenger of God, upon him be blessings and peace, called 'the battleground of deaths'. He also said: 'The reaping of my Nation is between sixty and seventy.' It was at this age that the Messenger of God died, upon him be blessings and peace (aged sixty-three), as did Abū Bakr, ʿUmar and ʿAlī, may God be pleased with them. As for ʿUthmān, may God be pleased with him, he lived past eighty.

God the Exalted has said: *Did We not grant you a life long enough for him who reflects to reflect therein? And the warner came to you.* [35:37] It is said that the age referred to is sixty, while the 'warner' is the Qur'ān or the Messenger, or grey hair. 'God has left no excuse to a man whom he allows to reach sixty' [*ḥadīth*], which means He has left him no way of excusing himself by saying that the end came too soon and his life was too short.

The lifespans of the [Muslim] Nation are among the shortest there have been. Some people in bygone nations lived near to or in excess of a thousand years. Some scholars have said that in some long-vanished communities puberty was reached at the age of eighty. It is also said that one of Adam's sons died aged two hundred years, and other people felt sorry for him for having had such a brief life; and that Abraham the Friend, upon whom be peace, was circumcised at the age of eighty at God's command. And it is related that when the Messenger of God, upon whom be blessings and peace, considered the lifespans of his nation short in comparison to other nations, he implored and beseeched God on their behalf, for if their days were short then their time spent in obedience and in preparation for their Hereafter would be short likewise, and they would thus miss many of the rewards and high degrees granted by God. So He gave him the Night of Destiny [*laylat al-qadr*], *which is better than a thousand months*, [97:3] thus [in effect] extending their lives and multiplying their rewards, so that any one of them who spends it in religious observance during this night will be as if he had done so for a thousand months: namely, for eighty-three years and four months. If he does this every Night of Destiny for twelve years, for instance, it would be as if he had lived one thousand or more years in God's obedience. Reflect on these calculations, for they are evident! This is what God has given this Nation through the *baraka* of His Messenger and the greatness of his honour in His sight, and because of the tremendous concern which the Prophet has, upon him be blessings and peace, for his Nation, and his zeal to see them obtain what is good.

In the age of seniority, people's dominant state is to revert to God, to be careful to gather provisions for their life-to-come, to renounce the things of the world, and do their utmost in obedience—when success in this is granted them. It is the age of dignity, reverence, and the total avoidance of jest and levity. Any person of this age not conforming to this pattern will be thought of as ugly of behaviour and reprehensible of conduct. In the authentic *ḥadīth* about the three [kinds of people] 'to whom God does not speak, look at, or purify on the Day of Rising, and who have a painful punishment', one of the three is 'the adulterous old man'. This abhorrent depravity is even more abhorrent and depraved in his case, because of his age and his supposed fear of God, apprehension, gravamen, and shame before God.[12]

White hair usually appears at this time. 'For someone whose hair turns grey while a Muslim, it becomes a light for him.' [*Ḥadīth*.] It has been related that the first person whose hair turned white was Abraham the Friend, peace be upon him, who asked: 'O Lord! What is this?' His Lord answered: 'This is dignity.' So he said: 'Lord, give me more dignity!'

White hair is a reminder of the nearness of one's time and

the necessity of folding up the spread carpet of hope. It proclaims the imminence of one's departure and rapidity of change. It is said that 'white hair brings with it the suspicion that one's time has come; it is the banisher of hope.'

Al-Khaṭīb ibn Nubāta said: 'White hair is a hole in life which cannot be plugged, and whose worsening is not repaired by time. It is a light that rises as the breath of life sets, a mover of people to the place of rotten bones. Do not — may God have mercy on you—burn the light of your white hair with the fire of your sins.'

The Messenger of God, upon whom be blessings and peace, has said: 'God the Exalted has said: "By My Eminence and Majesty, and the need of My creatures for Me, I would be too ashamed to torment My menservants and womenservants whose hair has turned white in Islam."' Then he wept, so that they asked: 'What is it that makes you weep, O Messenger of God?' And he replied: 'I weep because of those before whom God is ashamed and who do not feel ashamed before Him.'

A white-haired Muslim must be respected, for the Prophet has said, upon him be blessings and peace: 'It is part of revering God to revere a white-haired Muslim, the bearer of the Qur'ān, when he is neither excessive nor deficient regarding it, and the equitable leader [*imām*].' He also said: 'Someone who does not show respect for our elders and compassion for our youngsters, and does not enjoin good and forbid evil, is not of us.' And he said: 'Whenever a young man honours an older person, God sends him someone who will respect him when he reaches that age.' Imām al-Ghazālī, may God show him His mercy, has commented on this *ḥadīth* by saying that [to practice this virtue] contains good tidings of a long life, together with the reward such a life may contain.

Dying white hair with saffron or a red colouring is to be recommended, while black is prohibited except for those who fight in *jihād* for the sake of God, to put fear and apprehension into the unbelievers.

Decrepitude

One then passes from seniority to decrepitude, that time which, according to Ibn al-Jawzī, extends from seventy onward, when people become weak in all their senses, limbs, and faculties. *God is He Who created you out of weakness, then appointed after weakness strength, then after strength, appointed weakness and grey hair. He creates what He will; He is the Knower, the Able.* [30:54] Then one goes on to the 'worst time of life' [*ardhal al-ʿumur*]: *And among you there is he who is brought back to the worst time of life, so that, after knowledge, he knows nothing,* [22:5] which is senility and the loss of one's mental faculties. It is from this that the Messenger of God, upon whom be blessings and peace, asked God to protect him in his prayer: 'I ask for Your protection from being brought back to the worst time of life', or, in another *ḥadīth*, from 'the evil of senility'.

In the Psalms [*Zabūr*] it is written: 'Someone who reaches seventy suffers even when he is not ill.'

Ḥudhayfa ibn al-Yamān, may God be pleased with him, said: 'They said: "O Messenger of God! What are the ages of your nation?" and he replied: "Their deaths shall be between sixty and seventy." So they said: "O Messenger of God! And those over seventy?" And he replied: "Few of my nation will reach that age. May God have mercy on the over-seventy, and may God have mercy on the over-eighty!"'

The following are some poems on the subject:

If seventy is your sickness,
then you will find no doctor till you die.
Truly, a man who has reached seventy years,
is drawing near to his final resting place.

The man of seventy, and the ten beyond,
is not nearer than the one made wise by the next years
But has hopes, hoped by a man,
whose hopers are both right and wrong.

Whoever lives sees his zeal dimished by the days,
and his two trusty eyes and ears betray him.

The days go by one after the other,
and we are just driven to the graves while we watch.
Our youth which is gone shall never return,
neither shall these ruinous grey hairs depart.

The delight of life is health and youth,
and when they leave a man, they're gone.
When an old man grows weary, he is not tired of life
it is only of his weariness that he wearies.

Maʿan ibn Zā'ida once entered upon al-Ma'mūn, who asked him: 'Into what state has old age led you?' He replied: 'To stumbling on a lump of dung and being wounded by a hair.' He said: 'How are you with food, drink, and sleep?' He said: 'When I am hungry I am angry, but when I eat I am not content. I become drowsy in company, and sleepless when I go to my bed.' 'How are you with women?' 'The ugly among them I have no wish for, and the pretty among them have no wish for me.' Al-Ma'mūn finally said: 'The likes of you should not be on duty. Let him have twice as much provision and stay at home. Let people ride to him, and let him have to ride to no-one!'

Know that a long life in God's obedience is greatly to be desired. 'The best among you are those whose lives are long and whose works are good'. [*Ḥadīth.*] And: 'Let none of you wish for death, [for you are] either doing well and thus may increase, or doing evil and thus enjoying the chance to make amends.' However, as we mentioned before, the Prophet, upon whom be blessings and peace, sought God's protection against the 'worst age', namely, senility and mental disturbance.

Despite this, what is good in a lifetime is its *baraka*, and being granted success to do good works, both public and personal. God may put *baraka* into some of his chosen servants' short lives, which then become of more and wider benefit than the long lives of others. Such were Imām al-Shāfiʿī, God's mercy be upon him, for he died at the age of fifty-four. Imām al-Ghazālī, the Proof of Islam, died at fifty-five, the noble Quṭb Imām ʿAbdallāh ibn Abī Bakr al-ʿAydarūs Bā-ʿAlawī died at fifty-four, Imām al-Nawawī died before reaching fifty, while the righteous Khalīfa, Imām ʿUmar ibn ʿAbdal-ʿAzīz died before reaching forty. And there have been many other leaders from whom, despite their short lives, benefit and *baraka* spread widely through the world. *That is God's grace and He bestows it upon whom He wills.*

The Muḥammadan Nation has enormous *baraka*. It has a place in God's regard enjoyed by no other nation, while its people have shorter lifetimes, as a whole, than earlier nations, as we have said.

This last period, namely decrepitude, ends most commonly with a fatal illness, and—uncommonly—with death without illness. Infrequent as the latter is, it still does occur, and the Proof of Islam, when writing on long hopes and forgetting the imminence of one's appointed end said: 'If you say: "death occurs mostly after illness, and is rarely sudden" then you should know that death can indeed descend suddenly, and even if this does not happen, illness can also come suddenly, and when you are ill you become incapable of doing the good works which are one's travelling-provisions for the Hereafter.'

Know that cutting hopes short and remembering death often are desirable and recommended, while long hopes and being oblivious of death are repugnant. God the Exalted has warned against these things:

> *O you who believe! Let not your wealth or your children distract you from the remembrance of God. Those who do so: they are the losers. And spend of that with which We have provided you, before death comes to one of you and he says: 'My Lord! If only You would reprieve me for a little while, then I would give alms and be among the righteous!'*

> *But God reprieves no soul when its term has come, and God is aware of what you do.* [63:9–11]

> *Has the time not come for the hearts of those who believe to submit to God's reminder and to the truth which has been revealed? That they become not like those who received the Book of old, then the term was prolonged for them so their hearts were hardened; and many of them are depraved.* [57:16]

The Messenger of God, upon whom be blessings and peace, said: 'Remember often the Ender of Pleasures.' He was also asked: 'Shall anyone be resurrected among the martyrs who is not one of them?' and he replied: 'Yes, those who remember death twenty times each day and night.'

When he was asked who the intelligent were he replied: 'Those who remember death most often, and prepare for it best. They are the intelligent ones, who have gained the honour of this world and a noble rank in the Hereafter.' And he said: 'Death is the most imminent of all hidden things lying in wait.' Now, if death is the nearest of the hidden things lying in wait, then one must prepare for it through being decisive and taking the greatest precautions in every condition in which it may come. And this could be any time and under any circumstance.

The Proof of Islam, may God show him mercy, writes in his *Beginning of Guidance*: 'Know that death does not pounce at any specific time or situation, but that it is nonetheless certain to come. Preparing for it, therefore, takes precedence over preparing for the world.'[13] And he writes elsewhere in the same book: 'Do not abandon reflection on the imminence of your appointed time and the descent of death, which cuts off all hopes, when there will no longer be the possibility of making choices, when regrets and remorse will come as a consequence of having remained beguiled by illusion.'[14]

Among the righteous predecessors there were people who if they had been told: 'You are to die tomorrow', would not have found scope to increase their good works, so constantly were they addressing themselves to the Hereafter and occupying themselves with acts of goodness. One of them told a man who had asked him for advice: 'See which things which it would please you for death to find you doing them, and keep doing them now! And see which things which, were death to find you doing them, you would be displeased, and abandon them now!'

In a *ḥadīth* you will find: 'Be in the world as though a stranger or a wayfarer, and consider yourself one of the inhabitants of the graves,' and also: 'What have I to do with the world? The likeness of myself and the world is that of a rider travelling on a summer day, who found a tree, rested underneath it awhile, then went on, leaving it behind.'[15]

In remembering death often and feeling its imminence lie major benefits, some of which are: losing desire for the things of this world, being content with a little of it, persevering in acts of goodness (which represent provisions for the Hereafter), avoiding sins and transgressions, and being quick to repent of them should one commit them. Forgetfulness of death, and harbouring long hopes, result in the opposite of those benefits: strong desire for the world, greed in amassing its debris and enjoying its pleasures, being deceived by its decoration, postponing repentance of one's sins and laziness in doing acts of goodness.

Our righteous predecessors, may God show them His mercy, used to say: 'As hopes lengthen, behaviour worsens.' And the Prophet said, upon him be blessings and peace: 'The early members of this nation will be saved through renunciation [*zuhd*] and certitude, and the latecomers among them will perish because of greed and long hopes.' And ʿAlī, may God ennoble his face, said: 'That which I fear most for you is following your passions and harbouring long hopes, for following passions obstructs one from the Truth, while long hopes render you forgetful of the Hereafter.' There can be no good in hopes which cause us to forget the Hereafter, and it is this kind that the Messenger of God, upon whom be blessings and peace, sought protection from, saying: 'I seek

Your protection from every hope that distracts me.' And one of his prayers was: 'I seek Your protection from a worldly existence that prevents the good of the Hereafter, from a life that prevents a good death, and from a hope that prevents good acts.'

When the heart fills with the sensation that one will remain long in the world, then most of its attention will be devoted to making one's worldly affairs prosper, and one will become heedless of the Hereafter and of gathering provisions for it, until death takes one by surprise and one meets God bankrupt of good works. Then one will feel grief and remorse which are no longer of the least avail, and say: '*Would that I had sent before me* [*some provision*] *for my life*!' [89:24] and also: '*Lord! Send me back, that I may do right in that which I have left*!' [23:99–100]

Sickness and Death

When people fall ill, they should concentrate on asking abundantly for forgiveness, on remembering God, and on repenting of prior sins and times of forgetfulness, since they do not know whether this illness will lead to death, their time having come. They should therefore conclude their life with good works, 'for the worth of works lies in the final ones performed'. Sicknesses are reminders of the Hereafter and the return to God the Exalted. People should [at these times] make their legacies and give instructions, so that whatever needs to be done, whether for the Hereafter or for the world, is actually carried out, especially as regards anything that they owe other people, for these things are serious, and hard to extricate oneself from.

In their illness they should think exceedingly well of God the Exalted. 'Let none of you die without thinking well of God.' [*Ḥadīth*.] Let this be the dominant state of the heart, for God the Exalted says: 'I am as My servant thinks Me to be, and I am with him when he remembers Me'. [*Ḥadīth*.] He once entered, upon him be blessings and peace, the house of a sick young man to visit him, and asked him: 'How are you?' 'Hoping in my Lord,' he replied, 'and fearful of my sins.' And he declared: 'Never do these two things unite in the heart of a Muslim, in such a situation as this, but that God grants him what he hopes for, and gives him safekeeping from what he fears.'

Hope should be the predominant state in ill people, especially when the signs of impending death appear, so that they may die thinking well of God, hoping strongly for His generosity and the vastness of His mercy, and yearning to meet Him. 'Those who are pleased to meet God, God is pleased to meet them, and those who dislike to meet God, God dislikes to meet them. [*Ḥadīth*.] This is because a Muslim, when death is imminent, receives glad tidings of God's mercy and grace; he is therefore pleased to meet Him, and God is pleased to meet him. A hypocrite, on the other hand, when death is imminent, receives news of God's chastisement; he is therefore unhappy to meet Him, and God is unhappy to meet him. Thus believers who have *taqwā* receive glad tidings of God's mercy as they leave the world: their spirits, in their eagerness for their Lord and the meeting with Him, almost fly out of their bodies; they long for the instant when the angels will greet them and give them the tidings that they will enter the Garden and that [as of that instant] *neither fear will afflict them neither will they grieve.* [46:13]

God the Exalted has said:

> *Those whom the angels take [at death] in a goodly state, saying: Peace be upon you! Enter the Garden because of what you used to do.* [16:32]
>
> *Those who say: 'Our Lord is God' and then have rectitude; the angels descend upon them, saying: 'Fear not, nor grieve, but hear good tidings of the Garden which you were promised. We are your allies in the life of the world and in*

the Hereafter. There you will have what your souls desire, and there you will have that for which you pray. A gift of welcome from One Forgiving, Merciful'. [41:30]

Ill people should make sure that no impurities soil their bodies or clothes, thus preventing them from doing the Prayer [*Ṣalāt*]. Let them beware very greatly of abandoning the Prayer, for everyone can pray according to his condition, whether sitting, reclining, or in whatever way proves possible. Let them not conclude their works [in the world] by neglecting the Prayer, for it is the pillar of the religion. Any of their relatives or friends who happen to be there should encourage them to perform it, remind, and assist them. They should be aware that the obligation to pray remains in force for as long as one is conscious.

Let them frequently repeat these words: 'There is no god but You; Transcendent are You! I have been among the unjust' [*lā ilāha illā anta subḥānaka innī kuntu min al-ẓālimīn*], for it has been related that someone who repeats this forty times and then dies in his illness, dies as a martyr. Let them also recite *Sūrat al-Ikhlāṣ* in abundance. There are some phrases concerning which the Messenger of God, upon whom be blessings and peace, said the Fire would not feed on whoever repeated them in his illness and then died. Some of these are: *Lā ilāha illa'Llāh wa'Llāhu akbar, Lā ilāha illa'llāhu waḥdahu lā sharīka lahu lahu'l-mulku wa-lahu'l-ḥamd, lā ilāha illa'Llāhu wa-lā ḥawla wa-lā quwwata illā bi'Llāh.*

When the patient seems to be approaching death, those of his family and relatives who are present must watch him. If they notice signs of panic and terror they must remind him of his good works, the immensity of his Lord's mercy, His forgiveness of the sinful, and His pardon of people of remissness. Our predecessors encouraged such behaviour towards people on their deathbed, and some of them sought it from those present at the time of their own death.

It is a definite obligation that someone who is dying be encouraged to say *lā ilāha illa'Llāh*, for the Prophet said, upon him be blessings and peace: 'Make the dying say *lā ilāha illa'Llāh*, for someone whose last words are *lā ilāha illa'Llāh* will enter the Garden.' When the patient says it once it is not necessary that he be asked to repeat it, unless he speaks about anything else. They should also recite the *sūra* of *Yā-Sīn* to him. 'Recite *Yā-Sīn* to your dying'. [*Ḥadīth.*] It is said that this makes the departure of the spirit easier, for death, although accompanied by distress and throes, may be rendered easy and bearable to some believers. It is related that the Angel of Death, upon whom be peace, has said: 'I am compassionate with believers, and gentle.'

The dying may be subject to various kinds of temptation — and may God protect us!—and it is therefore recommended that the people who are present recite Qur'ān in abundance, and mention *ḥadīths* which condemn the things of the world. It has been related that Satan, may God curse him, is nearest to the servant at the time of his death, eager to tempt him, but that *his power is only over those who take him for an ally, and those who commit association.* [16:100] As for people of faith, *God confirms those who believe with the firm saying in the life of the world and in the Hereafter, and God sends the unjust astray, and God does as He wills.* [14:27]

The righteous Predecessors [*salaf*], may God have mercy on them, were very fearful of experiencing a bad ending [*sū' al-khātima*]. There are many stories relating to this, and some of them do indeed inspire great fear. The Messenger of God, upon whom be blessings and peace, said:

> By the One besides whom there is no other god! One of you might do the works of the people of the Garden, until only [separated from it] by an arm's length, and then that which had been written overtakes him and he does the works of the people of the Fire, and enters it. And one of you might do the works of the people of the Fire until nothing remains between him and it but an arm's length; then that which had been written overtakes him, he

> does the works of the people of the Garden, and so enters it.
>
> A man may seem to do the actions of the Garden's people, while he is one of the people of the Fire. And a man may seem to do the actions of the Fire's people, while he is one of the people of the Garden.

And there are many other *ḥadīth* with this message.

According to the ulema, those who are most in danger of ending badly—and may God protect us!—are those who are careless of their prayers, are habitual alcohol-drinkers, undutiful to their parents, inflict harm on other Muslims, or persist in committing major and mortal sins and fail to repent. *Then evil was the upshot of those who dealt in evil, because they denied the revelations of God, and made mock of them.* [30:10]

A Muslim should hope that through God's grace he will not be stripped of the blessing of Islam which had been granted to him from the outset through no effort of his own. He should fear its removal through his lack of gratitude for this blessing, which is the greatest blessing of all. There was once, among the predecessors, a man who swore by God that no-one ever feels completely secure regarding his Islam without being stripped of it. One should, therefore, continuously beseech God the Exalted, and implore Him to grant one a good ending. It is said that Iblīs, may God curse him, once declared: 'Someone who asks God for a good ending breaks my back, and I say: "Will he never become conceited because of his actions? I fear that he may have understood!"'

O Lord God! We ask You by the Light of Your Face, and by Your right over Yourself, [to grant us] a good ending at the time of death, for us, our loved ones, and for all the Muslims, O Most Merciful of the Merciful! *Lord, allow not our hearts to swerve after You have guided us; grant us of Your Mercy, You are the Bestower!* [3:8] *Lord make us patient, and take us to You as Muslims!* [7:126][16]

It is a *sunna* for the dying man to lie on his right side, facing the *Qibla*. When he breathes his last, his eyes should be closed, for at that time they will have become fixed upwards. '[A man's] gaze follows his spirit.' [*Ḥadīth*.] Those present must ask for much forgiveness and mercy for him and pray for him, for the angels will then say *Āmīn*. It is permitted to weep, but fortitude is better. As for wailing, lamentation, throwing dust on one's head, slapping one's cheeks, and rending one's clothes, these are all expressly forbidden, for many sound *ḥadīths* have banned them and warned those who do them.

Wishing for death is discouraged, and so is praying for it, if this be done by reason of difficulties such as sickness, poverty, or other worldly afflictions. If, however, it is because one fears to be tempted or afflicted in one's practice of religion, then it becomes permitted, and can sometimes even be recommended. 'Let none of you wish for death because of some hardship which has descended upon you. If you must, then say: "O Lord God! Give me life for as long as life is better for me, and cause me to die when death is better for me".' [*Ḥadīth*.] 'Let none of you wish for death, for one is either doing good, in which case one may gain, or doing evil, in which case one may repent'. [*Ḥadīth*.]

Death is inescapable for all. It is a decree which includes ordinary people and the elect; in which God has established equality between the powerful and the weak, the lowly and the noble; it is the power which conquered the Caesars and broke the Shahs. For believers He has rendered it a 'gift',[17] (and what a gift!), and an elevation (and what an elevation!), while for hypocrites it is regrets (and what regrets!), and defeat (and what a defeat!).

Glorified is He! The Sovereign, Compeller, Invincible; Who is Unique in having permanence and abiding, is High above death and extinction. He is the First without beginning, the Last without end. *All that is upon it shall pass away, and there shall remain the Face of your Lord, possessed of majesty and generosity*. [55:27] *Everything will perish save His Face. His is the judgment, and to Him you shall return*. [28:88] *Every soul shall taste of death, and you will be paid fully on the Day of Rising.*

Whoso is brought away from the Fire and made to enter the Garden: he has triumphed. The life of this world is but the comfort of illusion. [3:185]

Afterword

The following is related on the authority of Anas ibn Mālik, may God be pleased with him:

> The Messenger of God, upon whom be blessings and peace, said: 'For a newborn child until he reaches the age of discretion, his good deeds are written to the credit of his parents, while his bad deeds are written neither against him nor against his parents. Once he reaches the age of discretion and the pen begins to write [his acts], God the Exalted issues His command to the two angels who accompany him and guard and counsel him. When he reaches forty years in Islam, God gives him security from three [things]: madness, leprosy, and vitiligo.[18] When he reaches fifty, God makes his reckoning lighter. When he reaches sixty, God grants him to revert to Him as pleases Him. When he reaches seventy, the inhabitants of Heaven love him. When he reaches eighty, God records his good acts and is lenient with his bad ones. When he reaches ninety, God forgives him his bygone sins and those to come, allows him to intercede on behalf of the people of his family, and he becomes God's prisoner on the earth. Then, should he be *returned to the worst age, so that after having had knowledge he knows nothing*, God continues to record as good acts for him those which he used to do when he was well, and if he commits an evil act it is not recorded.'[19]

This *ḥadīth* is mentioned by Shaykh Aḥmad ibn ʿAlī ibn Abi'l-Qāsim al-Yamanī among the forty *ḥadīth* he has collected regarding the forgiveness of sins that had gone by and sins to come.

'A man dies in accordance with what he had lived in, and is resurrected in accordance with what he had died in'. [*Ḥadīth.*]

'When God wishes good for His servant, He wishes him up'. They said: 'How does He wish him up?' and he replied: 'He blesses him with success in doing good before he dies.' [*Ḥadīth.*]

And when a funeral procession once went by him the Prophet, may blessings and peace be upon him, said: 'Delivered or delivered from!' They asked: 'O Messenger of God! What is delivered, and what is delivered from?' He replied: 'God's believing bondsman is delivered from the hardship of the world and its harm into His Mercy. As for a depraved person: people, towns, trees and animals are delivered from him.'

And he said to Abū Dharr: 'O Abū Dharr! The world is the prison of the believer, the grave his place of safety, and the Garden his end. O Abū Dharr! The world is the Garden of the disbeliever, the grave is his torment, and the Fire his end.'

Ibn ʿAbbās, may God be pleased with him, said: 'If you see death nearing a man, give him good tidings, so that he may meet his Lord thinking well of Him, and if you see him well and alive, put fear into him.'

ʿAlī, may God be pleased with him, said: 'When a believer dies the place where he used to pray weeps for him, and so does the place from which his deeds used to ascend to Heaven.' Then he recited: *The heaven and the earth wept not for them.* [44:29]

And [the Prophet] said, may blessings and peace be upon him: 'Someone whose death coincides with the close of Ramaḍān enters the Garden, and someone whose death coincides with the close of ʿArafāt enters the Garden, and someone whose death coincides with the close of his charity enters the Garden.'

And he said: 'Someone who dies on a Thursday night or on a Friday is given a protection against the torment of the grave, and shall arrive on the Day of Rising with the marks of the martyrs.'

THE THIRD LIFE

The Intermediate Realm

The third life extends from the time a man leaves the *dunyā* at death until the moment he rises from his grave at the blowing of the Horn. This is the Intermediate Realm [*Barzakh*]. God the Exalted has said: *And behind them is a barzakh until the day when they are raised.* [23:100]

When a Muslim dies, and his death is confirmed, he has to be prepared for the grave. Thus he must be washed, shrouded, and prayed over [*janāza*], all of which must be done according to the Prophetic *Sunna*. His relatives, neighbours, and friends must be informed, and also the people of goodness and virtue, so that they may pray and ask mercy for him, and attend his funeral. It is recommended that whoever is informed of the death of his brother Muslim should say: 'We are God's and to Him we shall return'[20] and then: 'O God! Place his record in ʿIlliyyīn,[21] record him as a man of excellence [*muḥsin*], provide a successor for him in caring for his family in the ephemeral world, and forgive us and him, O Lord of the Worlds!'[22]

Next, one can pray some more for him, and praise him as a good man, for the Prophet has said, may blessings and peace be upon him: 'Mention the goodness of your dead, and refrain [from mentioning] their wickedness.' And there is another *ḥadīth* with the sense that: 'You are God's witnesses on earth, those whom you praise will be thus [i.e. praiseworthy].'[23] However, exaggerated praises bordering on or actually becoming lies are to be avoided.

The Intermediate Realm is the abode which lies between

the world and the life-to-come. It has more affinity with the latter, and is in fact a part of it. It is a place where spirits and spiritual things are predominant, while physical bodies are secondary but share with the spirits in their experiences, whether felicity and joy, or torment and grief.[24] Spirits endure, while bodies decay and gradually dissolve so that nothing remains except the lowermost tip of the spine, from which they will be formed anew at the Resurrection, as is recorded in *ḥadīth.* The exception is the bodies of the Prophets, upon them be blessings and peace, for they are alive in their graves, and so are the martyrs who died in God's path. *Do not think that those who are slain in the way of God are dead. Nay, they are living, with their Lord, provided for.* [3:169] 'Their spirits will be inside green birds who freely move in the Garden, and retire into lanterns attached to the Throne.' [*Ḥadīth.*] It has also been related that the souls of believers will be inside white birds which feed on the Garden's fruits.

Much reward lies in escorting funerals, praying for the dead and attending their burial. In a sound *ḥadīth* it is said: 'Anyone who escorts the funeral procession of a Muslim until he prays for him shall receive one measure of the reward. If he remains until he is buried, he receives two measures—and each measure is the size of Mount Uḥud.' And it has been said that whenever someone escorts the funeral of his brother Muslim, God orders the angels to escort his own funeral and pray over him when he dies.

It is recommended that people who have died be moved quickly to their graves. 'When a funeral procession is ready and the men lift him up, if the person had been righteous it says: "Advance! Advance!" If, however, the dead person had been otherwise it would say: "Woe is me! Where are you taking me?"' [*Ḥadīth.*] 'Make haste with the funeral procession. If he had been righteous, you are taking him on to goodness, whereas if he had been otherwise, it is an evil which you will unload from your necks.' [*Ḥadīth.*]

The dead person perceives and is aware of those who

wash, shroud, and bury him. It has been said that his spirit is held by an angel who stands near him and walks with it in his funeral, so that he hears all that is said about him, whether good or evil.

The Torment of the Grave

When he is laid out in his grave it is recommended that those who put him there say: 'In the name of God, and according to the religion of the Messenger of God.'[25] It is also recommended that those who are near the grave put three handfuls of dust on it, saying with the first: '*From it did We create you*' with the second: '*To it shall We return you*' and with the third: '*And from it shall We bring you forth another time*'. [20:55] Then dust should be very gradually and gently poured over him until the grave is filled and evened, after which the people present should remain for a while reading Qur'ān, and asking forgiveness and firmness for him, for according to a *ḥadīth* this is the time when he will be questioned by the two angels, Munkar and Nakīr, who are the grave's tormentors. They ask: 'Who is your Lord? What is your religion? Who is your Prophet?' Those whom God gives strength then say: 'My Lord is God, Islam is my religion, and Muḥammad is my Prophet.' But those whom God allows to swerve will be confused and hesitating, just as in the world they had been doubtful, tortuous, neglectful of God's orders, and prone to violate His prohibitions. They say 'Er! Er! I do not know!'—as has been mentioned in sound *ḥadīths*. They will then strike him, and his grave will tighten around him and fill with torture.

As for the firm believer, however, who was established in faith and observance during his life, he will be given good tidings by the angels, his grave will be spacious and filled with both light and delight, his good works will surround him: his prayers, fasts, charity, recitations of Qur'ān, and remembrance of God the Exalted; all these things will drive away any terrors or fears that may come near him. 'The grave is either one of the Garden's meadows or one of the Fire's pits.' [*Ḥadīth.*] 'I have never seen anything more terrifying than the grave'. [*Ḥadīth.*]

Whenever ʿUthmān ibn ʿAffān, may God be pleased with him, came near a grave he wept so much that his beard became wet. Someone once remarked to him that when he mentioned the Garden and the Fire he never wept as much, and he said: 'I heard the Messenger of God, may blessings and peace be upon him, say: "The grave is the first of the Hereafter's stages. If one is saved from it then what comes next is easier, but if one is not saved from it, then what comes next is even harder."'

The Messenger of God, may blessings and peace be upon him, said: 'The grave has an oppressive tightness, and were [it possible for] anyone to escape this, Saʿd ibn Muʿādh would have done so,'—for he is the one for whom the Throne of the All-Merciful shook.[26]

It is said that the torment of the grave is mostly the consequence of three things: slander, calumny, and not guarding oneself against being soiled with urine. There are two *ḥadīths* relating to this: 'Much of the grave's torment is from urine.' And there is the incident in which when the Messenger of God, may blessings and peace be upon him, heard two men being tormented in their graves, he asked for palm twigs and put them on their graves, saying that their suffering might be relieved to a certain extent for as long as they remained moist. He then remarked that they were being tormented, and not for committing anything major. One of them was had become used to calumny, and the other did not clean himself from urine.

He frequently asked protection, may blessings and peace be upon him, from the grave's torment, and urged others to include this in their supplications following the *tashahhud* of every ritual prayer, and in their evening and morning invocations. For the grave's torment is real, and so is its bliss:

bliss for the people of faith and obedience, torment for those of disbelief, hypocrisy, depravity, and rebellion. Each of the two groups differs in the intensity of bliss or torment in proportion to how they differed in the world in their doing those things which attract reward and bliss, or chastisement and torment.

Spirits are subject to the grave's bliss or torment much more than bodies, although both share in it. There are differences of opinion [among scholars], but the truth is, as we said, that both spirits and bodies are subject to the grave's bliss or torment.

How the Living may help the Dead

Praying for the dead, asking forgiveness for them, and giving charity on their behalf are some of the things God causes the dead in their graves to benefit from and be protected by. There are many *ḥadīths* about this, and many fine and virtuous people have witnessed it in their dreams. Saʿd ibn ʿUbāda, may God be pleased with him, once said to the Messenger of God, may blessings and peace be upon him: 'My mother's soul departed suddenly, and had she been able to speak she would have given alms. Would it bring benefit to her if I did so on her behalf?' 'Yes!' he replied. So he dug a well [for people to take water from] and said: 'This is on behalf of Saʿd's mother.'

And another man said: 'O Messenger of God! My parents have died; is there anything left with which I may be good to them?' And he replied: 'There are four things: praying and asking forgiveness for them, carrying out their promises, being good to their friends, and giving proper attention to those kinship bonds which could only have been attended to by them.'

And the Prophet said, may blessings and peace be upon him: 'Were it not for the living the dead would have been doomed'; in other words, because of the prayers and requests for forgiveness and for mercy which they receive.

And he said, may blessings and peace be upon him: 'My Nation is a nation covered with mercy. Its members enter their graves with sins like unto the mountains, and leave their graves having been forgiven because the living have asked forgiveness for the dead.'

It is related that the gifts of alms, prayers, and Qur'ānic recitation sent by the living to the dead reach them carried by the angels on plates of light, and adorned with silk handkerchieves, and they say to them: 'This gift is from so-and-so', and in this way they find joy and delight.

A dead man was once seen in a dream and, upon being questioned about his state, said that he had been greeted by an angel who attempted to burn his face with a flame held in his hand. But one of the living said: 'God have mercy on so-and-so!'—and the flame went out.

One of the greatest things which one may offer to the dead is to recite Qur'ān and send on the reward for it. This is of great benefit and *baraka*. The Muslims have agreed on this everywhere throughout the ages, the majority of scholars and virtuous people have recommended it, and there are *ḥadīths* to confirm this. Although these *ḥadīths* have weak chains of transmission, there is a principle, as the *ḥadīth* scholar al-Suyūṭī (may God show him His mercy) has said, that: 'Weak *ḥadīths* may be acted upon when they indicate acts of goodness.' And these are indeed acts of goodness.

All the Qur'ān is blessed and beneficial, but the most beneficial thing to offer to the dead is *Sūrat al-Ikhlāṣ* eleven times, and this has been seen in many blessed dreams. Each person should recite this noble *sūra* the said number of times, either each night, each day, or more, or less, or even only on Thursday night, and offer the reward to his parents, teachers, and all those who had rights over him.

He must not forget his dead ones when he prays, asks forgiveness, or gives alms, lest he in turn be forgotten after his death, for the one who remembers is remembered, and the one who forgets is forgotten. Benevolence goes ahead of you, and God allows *not the reward of those who have done good to be wasted.* [18:30]

Visiting Graves

You should know that it is recommended to visit graves. The Messenger of God, may blessings and peace be upon him, permitted this after having at first forbidden it. It contains benefits both for the living visitor and the dead person who receives the visit. The Prophet said, may blessings and peace be upon him: 'Visit graves, for they are a reminder of death.' And: 'I used to forbid you to visit graves, but now you should visit them. They render one able to do without the things of the world, and remind one of the Hereafter.' He also said: 'No man visits the grave of his brother and sits by it but that he [the dead man] finds solace in this, having his spirit restored to him until the visitor departs.' And he said: 'A dead [person] in his grave is never more comforted than when those that he loved in the world pay him a visit.'

When a visitor enters the cemetery or passes it by he should say: 'Peace on you, O place of believers. We are granted respite until tomorrow. That which you were promised has come to you, and we will, God willing, rejoin you. You are our predecessors and we are your followers. I ask God to give us and you wellbeing. O God, forgive us and them!'[27]

It is recommended to visit the cemetery on Thursday night, Friday, Friday night until sunrise, and on Monday, for it is said—and this is supported by various narrations—that the spirits of the dead return to their graves at those times.

The visitor must ask for forgiveness and mercy for them, read whatever Qur'ān he can and make over the reward to them; he should remember that soon he will go to the same end, and learn the lessons to be drawn from their condition.

When he visits the graves of his parents, relatives, or anyone else who had rights over him, he must sit with unhurried serenity, pray for them, and ask abundantly for forgiveness, for they rejoice at this, and are glad. When he visits the graves of righteous people he should pray in abundance, for prayers are answered at many such places, as has often been experienced. The tomb of Imām Mūsā al-Kāẓim, the son of Imām Jaʿfar al-Ṣādiq, is known in Baghdad as the 'Proven Medicine', that is, for prayers to be answered and worries to be relieved, and so is the tomb of Maʿrūf al-Karkhī, also in Baghdad. Some of the noble house of the ʿAlawī Sayyids used to sit at the tomb of our master al-Faqīh al-Muqaddam for such long periods, in the heat of the sun, that sweat could have been wrung from their clothes, while they, because of their profound concentration in prayer, were unaware of this. This is reported of Shaykh ʿAbdallāh ibn ʿAlī and others.

As for rubbing tombs and kissing them, these are distasteful practices which are to be discouraged. Even worse is the custom of circling around them.

Some have said that it is better, if possible, to stand facing the top of the [buried person's] head. They claim that the dead are more aware of those who are before their faces, but God knows best.

Know that the deeds of the living are shown to their dead families and relatives: if these deeds are good they rejoice and are optimistic, and they pray for them to have firmness and rectitude, but if these deeds are otherwise, they feel sad and hurt, and they pray for them to be guided and given success in doing good. The Messenger of God, may blessings and peace be upon him, has said: 'Your deeds are shown to your dead relatives and kin. If they are good they rejoice, and if they are otherwise they say: "O Lord God! Do not let them die before You guide them as You guided us!"'

And he said: 'Your deeds are shown to God on Mondays and Thursdays, and to the Prophets, fathers, and mothers on Fridays. They rejoice at your good deeds, and their faces grow in radiance and in light. Therefore fear God, and do not distress your dead!'

Afterword

Know that all creatures shall be assembled in the Intermediate Realm between the Two Blasts, for at that time not a single creature will remain alive. *The Horn is blown, and all who are in the heavens and earth fall down in a swoon, save him whom God wills.* [39:68]

This is the 'First Blast', at which all living creatures shall die, so that only God, the Living, the Self-Subsistent, remains. This is the first phase of the Rising. The second phase is when all the dead are returned to life, by the permission of God the Exalted: *Then it is blown another time, and there they stand, awaiting.* [39:68] Between the two Blasts are forty years.

As for those whom God excepts (*'save him whom God wills'*), there are many opinions as to who they are. Some commentators say that they are the Angels, others say they are the Prophets, others still claim that they are the martyrs (and this opinion is the preferable one); and views other than these also exist.

The Messenger of God, may blessings and peace be upon him, said: 'The Dajjāl will be raised among my Nation, and shall remain for forty.' The narrator of this account said that he did not know whether this meant forty days, months or years. 'Then God will send Jesus son of Mary, may blessings and peace be upon him, who will look like ʿUrwa ibn Masʿūd al-Thaqafi. He will stalk him, and destroy him.' Then people will live for seven years during which there will be no enmity between any two people. Then God will send a cold wind from the direction of Syria, and anyone with as much as an atom's weight of goodness (or—he may have said—'faith') remaining on the face of the earth will die, to the extent that if one of you should enter into the bowels of a mountain it will follow him there and kill him. Those who will remain will be the worst of people, moving as delicately as birds, wearing the skins of predatory beasts, recognising no good, disapproving of no evil, and Satan will appear to them, saying: 'Will you not obey my call?' They will answer: 'What then should we do?' He will command them to worship idols and as they do this their provision will come to them and their lives will be comfortable. Then the Horn will be blown, and all those who hear it will cock their heads to one side, listening, and the first to hear it will be a man puddling his camel's drinking-pond with clay, after which everyone will swoon. Then God will send down a drizzling rain, which will make the bodies grow. At the second Blast they will *stand, awaiting*, and it will be said: 'O people! To your Lord!' and, *'Let them stand, for they are to be questioned!'* [37:24] Then it will be said: 'Bring the Fire's contingent!' 'How many from how many?' 'From every thousand, nine hundred and ninety-nine!' And this will be the *day which renders children grey-haired* [73:17], *the day when it befalls in earnest.* [68:42]

And he said, may blessings and peace be upon him: 'The Hour will not come for as long as someone still says "*Allāh*".'

And he said, may blessings and peace be upon him: 'Evil people will remain, living like donkeys in chaotic depravity; it is upon them that the Hour shall come.'

And he said, may blessings and peace be upon him: 'God will grasp the earth on the Day of Rising, fold up the heavens in His right hand and say: "I am the King! Where are the kings of the earth?"'

And he said, may blessings and peace be upon him: 'God will fold up the heavens on the Day of Rising, take them in His right hand, then say: "I am the King! Where are the tyrants? Where are the arrogant?" He will then fold up the earth in His left hand and say: "I am the King! Where are the tyrants? Where are the arrogant?"'

And he said, may blessings and peace be upon him: 'Islam

will wear out, in the way a garment becomes worn out; until no-one will know what fasting, prayer, pilgrimage, or charity might be. The Book of God the Exalted will one night be taken up, so that not one verse will remain on earth. Some groups of people will remain in which old men and women will say: "We remember that our parents used to say *Lā ilāha illa'llāh*, and so we say it too."'

And he said, may blessings and peace be upon him: 'You will not see the Hour before you see ten preceding signs. The first will be the sun rising from the West, then the Smoke, then the Dajjāl, then the Beast, three sinkings into the ground, one in the East, one in the West, and one in the Arabian peninsula, the appearance of Jesus, upon whom be peace, then Jūj and Ma'jūj,[28] and the last will be a fire coming out of the Yemen, from the lower part of Aden.'

Know that knowledge of when the Hour will come is possessed only by God the Exalted. No-one else knows it. *Say: Knowledge of it is only with my Lord, He alone will manifest it in its time.* [7:187] *Indeed, with Him is the knowledge of the Hour.* [31:34]

Created beings may, however, know about those signs and conditions which indicate its imminent advent. Many of these, which are described in many sound *ḥadīths*, have already come about, and only the major ones such as the sun rising from the West, the Dajjāl (God curse him!), the Beast, and the coming of Jesus remain.

THE FOURTH LIFE

Judgement-day

The fourth life extends from the time when a person leaves his grave for the Resurrection and Gathering, until the moment when mankind enter the Garden or the Fire.

God, Who is High and Majestic, shall command Isrāfīl, upon whom be peace, to blow the Horn a second time: *And the Horn is blown, and lo, from their graves they hasten to their Lord!* [36:51] *Then it is blown another time, and there they stand, awaiting.* [39:69] *Those who disbelieve claim that they will not be raised again. Say: 'Nay, by my Lord! You will be raised again, and then you will be informed of what you did, and that is easy for God'.* [64:7] *Your creation and your resurrection were only as a single soul. God is Hearer, Knower.* [31:28] *Have they not seen how God originates creation, then reproduces it? For God, that is easy. Say: Walk the land and see how He originated creation, then God brings forth the later growth. Indeed God is Able to do all things.* [29:19–20] *That is because God, He is the Truth, and because He quickens the dead, and He is Able to do all things. And because the Hour will come, there is no doubt about it, and God will raise those who are in the graves.* [22:6–7] *And of His signs is that you see the earth lowly, but when We send down water on it, it thrills and grows. Indeed He who quickened it is the Quickener of the Dead. He is Able to do all things.* [41:39] *And he gave us an example, forgetting his own creation, and said, Who will revive bones which have rotted away? Say: He will revive them Who first originated them; and He has knowledge of every creation.* [36:78–9]

Abū Razīn al-ʿUqaylī, may God be pleased with him, said: 'I once asked, "O Messenger of God! How does God originate creation, and what is the sign of that in His creation?" He replied: "Have you never crossed your people's valley when it was barren, then crossed it again when it was swaying with greenery?" I said: "Indeed I have!" And he told me: "That is His sign in His creation".'

In his book called *The Memorial*, al-Qurṭubī, may God show him His mercy, mentions a long *ḥadīth* narrated by Abū Hurayra, may God be pleased with him, who said: 'The Messenger of God, may blessings and peace be upon him, once spoke to us, a group of his Companions.' And he narrated the *ḥadīth* until he came to His saying (Majestic is His praise!): *On the day when the earth shall be changed to other than the earth, and the heavens, and they will come forth before God, the One, the Invincible,* [14:48] after which he said that the Messenger of God continued thus:

> He will level it, then spread it just as an ʿUkāẓī[29] leather rug is spread, *so that you will see neither crookedness nor curvature.* [20:107] God will then drive the people *in one cry,* [79:13] and they will be in the changed earth in the same state they had been in before, those who were inside it will be inside it, and those who were on its surface will be on its surface. Then God will send down upon you from beneath the Throne water called The Life [*al-Ḥayawān*], and it shall rain for forty days, until the water has risen twelve arm-lengths above you. Then He will give His command to the bodies, which will grow just as plants and vegetables grow, until, when your bodies are as fully formed as they had been, God the Exalted shall declare: 'Let the Bearers of the Throne return to life!'—and this will take place—then: 'Let Gabriel, Mīkā'īl, and Isrāfīl come back to life!' And Isrāfīl will be commanded to take the Horn,[30] after which God the Exalted will call the spirits, which will be brought to Him, the Muslims glowing with light, the others dark, and He will cast them into the Horn, then say

> to Isrāfil: 'Blow the Resurrection-Blast!' He blows, and the spirits fly out like bees, filling the space between heaven and earth, and God will say: 'By My Might and Majesty! Let each spirit return to its body!' And the spirits will repair to their bodies, enter through the nostrils, and spread as venom spreads in a man who is bitten. Then the earth shall split apart from around you, and I shall be the first for whom it shall do so. You will emerge as young people of thirty-three, while the language on that day will be Syriac. Quickly *they hurry to their Lord.* [36:50] *Hastening toward the Summoner, the disbelievers saying: This is a hard day.* [54:8] *That is the day of emerging.* [50:42] *And we assemble them and leave not one of them.* [18:47]

It has been mentioned in *ḥadīth* that humans rot away entirely, with the exception of one bone, the tip of the sacrum, which is a tiny bone at end of the spine. When God, Who is of mighty Ability, wishes to resurrect mankind, the sky pours down a rain which resembles male sperm, after which they grow from the places where they were buried, in the way that crops grow. Then He resurrects Isrāfil, upon whom be peace, and commands him to blow the Horn for the Resurrection. The spirits will then be returned to their bodies and brought back to life, by the leave of God the Exalted. The earth splits open to let them out, graves are overturned, and the bodies and spirits are summoned to stand before God the Exalted, at the Standing-Place of the Resurrection: *And on the day when We cause the mountains to move, and you see the earth emerging, and We assemble them and leave not one of them, and they are set before their Lord in ranks. 'You have come to Us as We created you at first. But you thought that We would set no time for you'.* [18:47–8][31] *On the day when the earth splits from around them, hastening forth; that is a gathering easy for Us.* [50:44]

The Messenger of God, may blessings and peace be upon

him, said: 'A man dies in accordance with what he had lived in, and is resurrected in accordance with what he had died in'.

He also said: 'Mankind shall be resurrected barefoot, naked, and uncircumcised, with women mixing with the men.' At this, ʿĀ'isha, may God be pleased with her, exclaimed: 'O shame! Each looking at the other!' And he replied: "The situation will be too desperate for them to be worried by that."'

And he said, may blessings and peace be upon him: 'People shall be gathered more hungry than they had ever been, more thirsty than they had ever been, more naked than they had ever been, and more exhausted than they had ever been. Those who had given food for God's sake will be fed by Him, those who had given drink for God's sake will be given to drink by Him, those who had given clothes for God's sake will be clothed by Him, and those who had acted for God's sake will be protected by Him.'

Once they are out of their graves they shall be ordered to walk to the place of gathering, which, it is said, will be the blessed and holy land in Syria,[32] towards which they will be driven by the angels. It has also been related that God will cause a fire to come from the lower part of Aden (or in another version, from a valley called Barhūt, which is in the south of Ḥaḍramawt) which will drive the people toward the land of the gathering. It will accompany them wherever they walk, stop when they rest, and will be with them evening and morning, moving at the pace of camels.

People will then see their deeds appearing before them: good ones will comfort and accompany them, wicked ones will reproach them and make them feel desolate. They may even climb on their backs and force them to carry them: *They bear their burdens upon their backs. Evil is that which they bear!* [6:31] *They will surely bear their own loads and other loads beside their own, and they will surely be questioned on the Day of Rising concerning that which they had invented.* [29:13]

Each person will be accompanied by his Recording Angels, who had taken down all his actions in his worldly life: *And every soul comes, along with it a driver and a witness.* [50:21]

Evil deeds committed in the world by people who died unrepentant will become manifest upon them: usurers[33] for instance will see their stomachs grow so large that as they walk, they are constantly overbalanced by their weight and stumble over. Adulterers will see their genitals swell so large that they will have to drag them along on the ground. Alcohol-drinkers will come to the Gathering with their cups in their hands. Liars, backbiters and slanderers will see their tongues lengthen until they reach their chests. Those who withheld their *Zakāt* will have their money made manifest in the shape of large snakes coiled around them. The arrogant will be brought in the form of small ants trodden both by the good and the depraved. And so shall it continue. *The guilty will be known by their marks, and will be seized by the forelocks and the feet.* [55:41]

Three groups of people, described in *ḥadīth*, are to be gathered [on the Day of Rising]: those who will ride, those who will walk on their feet, and those who will walk on their faces. For 'the One who made them walk on their feet is capable of making them walk on their faces.'

Muʿādh ibn Jabal, may God be pleased with him, said: 'I once asked, "O Messenger of God! What of the saying of God, the High and Majestic: *On the day when the Horn is to be blown, and you shall come in hosts*?" And the Prophet, may blessings and peace be upon him, said: "O Muʿādh ibn Jabal, you ask about a formidable thing!" Then he wept abundantly, and said: "Ten different kinds [of people] of my nation will be gathered in groups distinct from the groupings of the Muslims. Their forms will have been changed: some will have the forms of monkeys, others the forms of pigs, others will be upside down, their legs upwards, being dragged on their faces. Some will be blind, hesitant. Others will be deaf and dumb, lacking in reason; others still will be chewing their tongues which will hang on their chests, and their saliva will be pus, so that they disgust the other people of the gathering. Some will have their hands and feet cut off, some will be crucified on tree-trunks of fire, some will be fouler than putrid cadavers, and some will wear flowing robes of tar. As for those whose forms resemble monkeys: they are the slanderers. Those who have the forms of pigs are the people of ill-gotten, illicit, and unlawfully taxed money. Those whose heads and faces are beneath them are those who consumed usury. The blind are those who ruled tyrannously. The deaf and dumb are those who were proud of their actions. Those who chew their tongues are the ulema and judges whose conduct differed from their words. Those whose hands and feet are cut off are those who injured their neighbours. The people crucified on trunks of fire are those who frequently denounced people to the authorities. Those fouler than putrid cadavers are those who enjoyed passions and pleasures but withheld God's due in their wealth. And those who wear the robes are the arrogant, the boastful, and the conceited."' (Related by al-Qurṭubī, may God show him His mercy, in his *Memorial*.)

The Messenger of God, upon whom be blessings and peace, said: 'People will be gathered in a shining white land resembling pure flour, where there will be signs for no-one.'

And he said, may blessings and peace be upon him: 'Mankind will be gathered on a single plain, each will hear the Summoner, and eyesight will be penetrating.'

This is the 'standing-place' [*mawqif*] of the Day of Rising, where all creatures will be assembled: jinn, men, devils, cattle, wild beasts, and predators. Then the angels, upon whom be peace, shall descend to them at God's command, and surround them, rank upon rank, and the criminals and the unjust will find no place to flee. God has said: *O company of jinn and men, if you have power to penetrate all regions of the heavens and the earth, then do so! You will never penetrate them save with* [*Our*] *sanction. Which is it, of the favours of your Lord, that you deny? There will be sent against you flames of fire and brass, and you will not escape.* [55:32–5]

The gathering-place will become crowded: there will be

jostling and turmoil, and the sun will draw near until it is one mile above their heads. (The narrator of this account remarked that he did not know whether this would be a mile in distance, or the 'mile' which is the furthest that can be seen.)[34] Then people will be afflicted by great hardship, such heat and thirst that only God knows of: they will perspire until their sweat penetrates the earth to a depth of seventy arm-lengths. The Prophet said, may blessings and peace be upon him: 'The sun will come near the earth on the Day of Rising, and people will sweat. There will be some whose sweat will reach up to their heels, some for whom it will reach the middle of their legs, some to their knees, some to their thighs, some to their waists, some to their mouths' — here he raised his hand to his mouth—'and some will be [completely] covered by their sweat'—and he put his hand above his head.

He also said, may blessings and peace be upon him: 'A man will be under the shade of his charity on the Day of Rising.'

And he said: 'Seven [kinds of people] will be shaded by God under His Shade on the day when no shade will exist save His: a just leader, a young man who grew up in the worship of God, a man whose heart was attached to the mosques, two men who had love for each other in God, came together in this and separated in it, a man who, when a woman of rank and beauty attempted to seduce him, said: "I fear God!", a man who concealed his charity so that his left hand did not know what his right hand spent, and a man who remembered God when alone, and whose eyes overflowed with tears.' The meaning of 'His shade' here is 'the shade of His Throne'.

And he said: 'Whoever reprieves an insolvent man, or agrees to reduce his debt, will be shaded by God under His shade.'

And he said: 'Whoever wishes to behold the Day of Rising, let him recite: *When the sun...* [81:1] and: *When the heaven is split asunder...* [84:1]

When mankind's standing at this place is prolonged and

their hardship becomes overwhelming, they debate among themselves to decide whom they should go to who might intercede on their behalf, so that their Lord would pass judgement on them and they would be delivered from their situation. So they go to Adam, upon whom be peace, and he in turn sends them to Noah, upon whom be peace, who sends them on to Abraham, upon whom be peace. Abraham refers them to Moses, upon whom be peace, who sends them on to Jesus, upon whom be peace, and Jesus sends them on to Muḥammad, upon whom be blessings and peace. And Muḥammad says: 'I am [the one] for this. I am [the one] for this.' He goes to his Lord, asks His permission, then prostrates himself before Him and praises Him, and He bids him raise his head, and tells him to intercede, for he has been granted intercession. The *ḥadīths* regarding this are sound and well-known. It is said that this is the 'Praiseworthy Station' [*al-maqām al-maḥmūd*] which the first and the last of mankind envy him: *It may be that your Lord will raise you to a praiseworthy station.* [17:79]

It has come down to us that Muslim children who die before puberty will be permitted to give their parents to drink. They will move through the crowd searching for them at a time when thirst will be at its utmost. Once, a righteous man who had resolved never to marry saw in a dream that he was at the standing-place on the Day of Rising, thirsty beyond description, and there were children with water-bowls in their hands which they gave to some people but not to others. He asked them to let him drink, but they answered: 'We only give water to our parents'. In the morning he asked to be married, in the hope that God might bestow a child upon him, and that were that child to die he would be given to drink in that aweful situation. We ask God for His kindness, and for wellbeing through His grace. Āmīn!

Distress and terror will increase to such an extent that the disbelievers will say: 'O Lord! Release me, even if it be to the Fire!' When the Messenger of God, upon whom be blessings and peace, intercedes with his Lord, asking for judgement to be passed and the people to be released, He will issue His command to the angels who carry the Tremendous Throne, and they will carry the Throne of the All-Merciful to the Standing-Place. The Garden is then brought to the right of the Throne, and the Fire to the left, and mankind will be brought before God to be judged. Some will be subjected to no reckoning at all—and these are the Foremost [*al-sābiqūn*]; some will be gently called to account, and others harshly, and anyone who will be harshly questioned will [inevitably] be tormented. Some will be given their books in their right hands, some in their left, and some behind their backs.

God the Exalted shall ask the Messengers about their communication of the Message to their nations, and shall ask those nations whether the Messengers had conveyed it: *Then We shall question those to whom [Our message] was sent, and We shall question the Messengers. With knowledge shall We speak to them, and never were We absent.* [7:6] Some faces will become white and some will grow black. *On the day when some faces will be whitened and others blackened. As for those whose faces have been blackened, it will be said unto them: Did you disbelieve after your [profession of] faith? Then taste the punishment for having disbelieved. And as for those whose faces have been whitened, they dwell in the mercy of God for evermore.* [3:106–7]

All people will be made to stand before God to be questioned about their deeds. The Messenger of God, upon whom be blessings and peace, said: 'There is not one of you who will not be spoken to directly by God, with no interpreter between them. You shall look to the right and see nothing but that which you had sent ahead, to the left and see nothing but that which you had sent ahead, before you and see nothing but the Fire before your face. So protect yourself from the Fire, even with [as little as] half a date [as charity].'

And he said: 'The feet of a man will not move [from the Standing-Place] until he is questioned about four things: his youth and how he spent it, his life and how he used it, his wealth, how he earned it and how he spent it'—and in one version [of the *ḥadīth*]: 'and his actions, what they were'.

This is the time when people's tongues, hands, feet, and skins shall bear witness as to what they did. It has been suggested that the 'skins' [*julūd*] meant here are the genitals. *On the day when their tongues, their hands and their feet testify against them as to what they used to do.* [24:24] *This day We seal up their mouths, and their hands speak to Us, and their feet bear witness as to what they used to earn.* [36:65] *And they say to their skins: Why do you testify against us? They say: God has given us speech, even He Who gives speech to all things.* [41:21]

Similarly, each place on earth shall testify as to what they had done on it, whether good or evil. God the Exalted said: *That day it will relate its news.* [99:4] The Messenger of God, upon whom be blessings and peace, said: 'Do you know what its 'news' are? It will testify against each of God's slaves, man or woman, [and relate] what they have done. It will say: he did such-and-such a thing on such-and-such a day.' And the *ḥadīth* continues.

He also said, as reported by Ibn ʿUmar, may God be pleased with him: 'God will draw His believing slave nearer [to Him] until He shelters him; then He will ask him about his sins, and he will keep confessing [to one after another] until when he fears that he is lost, He will say: "I concealed them for you in the world, and I shall forgive you for them today".'

This prolonged and hard situation may be made easier for the devout believer; [it may be shortened to the extent that] it becomes only as long as [the time taken to perform] an obligatory prayer, or, in another version, the time between the noon and afternoon prayers. This has been affirmed in a *ḥadīth*.[35]

One of the most distressing situations for mankind at the Standing-Place shall be when God orders the Fire to be brought, led by seventy thousand halters, each halter held by seventy thousand angels. When it comes near to mankind and they hear its breathing, its roars, and other terrifying and hideous noises, they will fall to their knees. Even the Prophets will become fearful, and the innocent will be afraid, to the extent that each of the noble Messengers, may peace be upon them, will say: 'O Lord! Myself! Myself! I beseech You for no-one else!' The exception shall be God's Messenger, upon whom be blessings and peace, who will keep saying: 'My nation! My nation!' It has been related that he will advance towards the Fire and drive it back from mankind. It has been ordered to obey him, and will allow the angels holding its halters to take it to the left of the Throne.

The reckoning is recorded, and every creature is given its due, even the cattle. It has been said that the hornless goat shall exact its retribution from the horned one. Then, when the animals have received their dues from each other, God will say to them: 'Become dust!' At that *the disbeliever will say: 'Would that I were dust!'* [78:40]

The Balance and the Bridge

Then the Balance [*Mīzān*] shall be erected for the weighing of deeds. As God the Exalted has said: *And We set a just balance for the Day of Rising, so that no soul is wronged in anything. Though it be the weight of a mustard grain, We bring it forth, and sufficient are We as Reckoners.* [21:47] *The weighing that day is true. As for those whose scales are heavy, they are the triumphant. And as for those whose scales are light, they are those who have lost their souls because of the wrong they used to do to Our revelations.* [7:8–9]

Good and evil deeds shall both be weighed. Those people whose good acts outweigh the bad are the victors and the fortunate, while those whose evil ones outweigh the good have lost and failed. As for those whose good and evil deeds are equal, it is said that they will be stood on the *Aʿrāf* between the Garden and the Fire, after which, through God's

Mercy, they will go on to the Garden. It is related that there will be an angel standing at the Balance, who, when the balance is heavy, will announce: 'So-and-so, son of so-and-so, has a heavy balance; he will be in such bliss as will never be followed by hardship!' And when the balance is light he will proclaim: 'So-and-so, son of so-and-so, has a light balance; he will suffer and never know happiness again!'

The Bridge [*Ṣirāṭ*] shall be thrown across Hell and mankind will be ordered to cross it. It is related that it will be sharper than a sword, narrower than a hair, and that people will have to cross it with their deeds. Those whose faith is more perfect and who were quicker to obedience, will be light, and shall cross as [swiftly as] lightning. [Others will be] like the wind, others like birds, others like the best of horses, others like riders, others like strong men burdened by their deeds, others will go on hands and knees, some will be scorched by the Fire, and others will tumble into it. The first to cross will be the Messengers, may blessings and peace be upon them, each of them saying: 'O Lord! Save! Save!' The very first to cross will be Muḥammad, upon whom be blessings and peace; while the first nation to cross shall be his.

Trustworthiness and Kinship-bonds will be sent to stand by the Bridge. It will be moist and slippery, and will have hooks like the thorns on the Saʿdān bush, which will take whoever they are ordered to take.

The Ḥawḍ

Then the believers will reach the *Ḥawḍ* ['lake'] of the Messenger of God, upon whom be blessings and peace. They will drink from it and their thirst will vanish. Its water will be whiter than milk, more fragrant than musk, and sweeter than honey. It will have two channels bringing water from the [river] Kawthar. Its breadth will be one month's journey, its length likewise, and around it will be pitchers [as numerous] as the stars in the sky. Anyone who drinks one sip from it will never thirst again.

The ulema have differed over whether the *Ḥawḍ* will be after the Bridge and before entering the Garden, or before the Balance and the Bridge. Both of these are possible.

This nation will be recognized among the nations because they will be shining from the effects of the *wuḍū'*-ablution, as is stated in a *ḥadīth*. Some people will be driven away from the *Ḥawḍ* after the Messenger of God, upon whom be blessings and peace, has seen and recognized them. They will be taken to the left side, and when he says: 'They are from among my companions!' he will be answered: 'You do not know what they did after you!'

The Intercession

The intercession [*shafāʿa*] will then become permitted, and the Prophets, the True Ones [*Ṣiddīqūn*], the ulema, the righteous, and the believers will intercede, each according to his rank with God the Exalted. A man of this nation will intercede for [a number as large as the flocks of] Rabīʿa and Muḍar[36], while others will intercede for just one or two people.

The first to be permitted to intercede shall be Muḥammad, upon whom be blessings and peace, who has said: 'I am the first to intercede and the first to be permitted intercession.' He is the greatest in rank among Prophets, and his is the greatest intercession. He will intercede many times, the first and weightiest of which shall be at the Judgement; and regarding this he has said: 'I shall continue to intercede until I am granted the release of people who had already been designated for the Fire.' And: 'I will continue to intercede until it will be said to me: "You have left no trace of your Lord's wrath in your nation."'

Among his many intercessions will be one for members of his nation who will have actually entered the Fire, so that they will be taken out of it, and for others who will have their degrees in the Garden raised, and so on until he will say to his Lord: 'Will You permit me [to intercede for] everyone who ever said *lā ilāha illa'Llāh*?'

And He – Sublime is He! – will declare to him: 'To do that is not for you; but by My might, I shall not let those who believed in Me one day in their life be like those who did not believe in Me at all!' This perhaps refers to those people of the Fire whom the Most Merciful will take out with His Hand — but God knows best.

Abū Hurayra, may God be pleased with him, related that he asked the Messenger of God, upon whom be blessings and peace, who would be most blest with his intercession on the Day of Rising, and he replied: 'The people most blest with my intercession shall be those who said *lā ilāha illa'Llāh*, sincerely and without being prompted.'

Zuhar ibn Arqam, may God be pleased with him, related that God's Messenger, may God bless him and grant him peace, said: 'Whoever says *lā ilāha illa'Llāh* with sincerity shall enter the Garden.' Someone asked: 'O Messenger of God! What does 'sincerity' in this involve?' And he replied: 'That it should restrain him from the things God has forbidden.'

Anas, may God be pleased with him, said that he once asked the Messenger of God, upon whom be blessings and peace, to intercede for him on the Day of Rising, and he replied: 'I shall do that, God willing.' So he asked him where he should seek him and he replied: 'You should first seek for me at the Bridge.' He said: 'And if I do not find you at the Bridge?' and he replied: 'Then at the Balance.' And he asked again: 'What if I do not find you at the Balance?' and he said: 'Then at the *Ḥawḍ*. I shall be found nowhere but at these three places.'

The Righting of Injustice

Know that one of the most difficult things on the Day of Rising is to have treated people unjustly, for injustice is something which God does not overlook. In a *ḥadīth* injustice is said to be of three kinds: one that is never forgiven by God, namely polytheism [*shirk*], one that is never overlooked by God, namely people's injustice to each other, and one that is disregarded by God, namely a person's injustice to himself in that which is between him and his Lord.

The Messenger of God, upon whom be blessings and peace, said: 'Do you know who the bankrupt are in my nation?' They said: 'Bankrupt people according to us are those who have neither money nor property.' But he said: 'The bankrupt of my nation are those who will come on the Day of Rising having prayed, fasted, and given *Zakāt*, but who have insulted this one, slandered that one, taken someone's wealth, or beaten him up. This one will be given of his good deeds and that one will be given of his good deeds; and if his good deeds are exhausted before all his debts are thus settled, he will be given some of their sins, which will be cast upon him; then he will be thrown into the Fire.'

It has been said that some people will be pleased to find on the Day of Rising that their fathers or their brothers owe them such debts, so that they will demand of them and cause them much distress. 'Let those who wronged their brothers set those wrongs aright before that Day comes when there will be neither dinar nor dirham, but only good and evil deeds. If they have good deeds, these will be taken away from them; and if not, then the evil deeds [of the wronged] will be cast upon them, and then they will be thrown into the Fire.' [*Ḥadīth.*]

Know that the Day of Rising is a formidable day. *Do such* [people] *not think that they will be resurrected, for a formidable day, the day when mankind stands for the Lord of the Worlds?* [83:4–6] Its hardships are protracted, and its terrors great. It has been described in a terrifying manner and at some length by God in His Mighty Book, and by the Messenger of God, upon whom be blessings and peace. The righteous predecessors, also, described it as they learnt of it from that which was transmitted to them from God and His Messenger. The ulema have compiled many volumes on the subject, for example the volume on 'Death and What Follows' in the *Iḥyā'*[37] and *The Precious Pearl which Reveals the Knowledges of the Hereafter*,[38] both by Ḥujjat al-Islām al-Ghazālī (may God show him His mercy), *The Memorial* by al-Qurṭubī,[39] and two volumes by as-Suyūṭī (may God show him His mercy), namely *The Opening of Hearts: Explaining the State of the Dead and the Graves*, and *Unveiled Moons: The Conditions of the Hereafter*.[40] We have mentioned here the main events and topics, giving a summary of those essentials of the subject of which has to be aware. People who wish to confine themselves to this will find it sufficient, while those who wish for more should read those books that we have mentioned, and other similar ones which we have not. And assistance and success come from God.

Afterword

The Messenger of God, upon whom be blessings and peace, said: 'For whoever relieves a Muslim's distress in this world, God shall grant him relief from one of the distresses of the Day of Rising. And whoever shields a Muslim will be shielded by God both in this world and in the Hereafter.'

And he said: 'Each Prophet has one prayer which must be answered. They have prayed, but I have concealed my prayer, so that it may be an intercession for my nation, including, God willing, all those who died without empartnering anything to God.'

And: 'If you wish, I will tell you of the first thing that God will say to the believers on the Day of Rising, and of the first thing they will say to Him.' They responded: 'Please do, O

Messenger of God!' and he said: 'He will ask the believers: "Were you eager to meet Me?" "Yes, Lord!" they will reply. He will ask: "Why was that?" and they will say: "We hoped for Your forgiveness, mercy, and good-pleasure." He will then say: "I shall make My mercy certain to be given you".'

And: 'When God created the Garden, He sent Gabriel there and told him: "Behold it, and behold what I have prepared there." He went and looked, and beheld what God had prepared there for its people. Then he went back and said to Him: "By Your Might! None will ever hear of it but that he will enter it!" So He ordered it to be surrounded with unpleasant things, and said: "Return, and look at what I have prepared in it for its people!" He returned, and, when he found it surrounded with unpleasant things, came back and said: "By Your Might! I fear that none will enter it!" And He said: "Go to the Fire, behold it, and see what I have prepared therein for its people!" And its parts were boiling over each other. He returned to Him and said: "By Your Might! No-one who hears of it will enter it!" So He ordered it to be surrounded with pleasures, and said: "Return to it!" He said: "By Your Might! I fear that no-one will be saved from it!"'

And: 'The one among the people of the Fire who had been living most luxuriously in the world will be brought on the Day of Rising and will dip his finger into the Fire. Then he will be asked: "O son of Adam, have you ever seen any goodness at all, has any kind of pleasure ever come to you?" He will reply: "No, by God, O Lord!" And the one among the people of the Garden who was most miserable in the world will be brought and will dip his finger into the Garden. Then he will be asked: "O son of Adam, have you seen any misery at all, has any kind of hardship ever befallen you?" And he will answer: "No, by God! I have never been through any misery at all, nor has any kind of hardship ever befallen me".'

ʿĀ'isha, may God be pleased with her, once remembered the Fire, and she wept. The Messenger of God, upon whom be blessings and peace, asked why she was weeping, and she replied: 'I remembered the Fire, and so I wept. Will you remember your family on the Day of Rising?' And he answered: "There are three situations where no-one can remember anyone: at the Balance until he knows whether his balance is light or heavy, at the record when it is said: "*There! Read my record!*" until he finds out whether his record will be placed in his right or left hand, or behind his back, and at the Bridge when it is cast across the Fire.'

And he has said, may blessings and peace be upon him: 'After the people of the Garden have gone to the Garden, and the people of the Fire have gone to the Fire, death will be brought between the Garden and the Fire, and will be slaughtered. Then a herald will proclaim: "O people of the Garden! Death is no more! And, O people of the Fire! Death is no more!" At this, the people of the Garden will become even more joyous, and the people of the Fire will become even more sorrowful.'

And: 'The people of the Garden shall be of one hundred and twenty parts: eighty from this nation and forty from all other nations.'

And: 'I have seen nothing like the Garden, whose seeker sleeps, nor like the Fire, whose fleer sleeps.'

And: 'Someone who fears sets out at nightfall, and someone who sets out at nightfall will reach the resting-place. Indeed the merchandise of God is precious. Indeed the merchandise of God is the Garden.'

And: 'I shall be the first of men to come out when they are resurrected. I shall be their leader when they arrive. I shall be their orator as they listen. I shall be their intercessor when they are detained. I shall be their giver of good tidings when they despair. Honour and the keys will on that day be in my hand. The Flag of Praise on that day will be in my hand. I am the dearest of the children of Adam to my Lord. One thousand servants will move around me, *like hidden pearls*, or *scattered pearls*.'

May God's blessings and peace be upon him, and may He increase him in favour, honour, and rank in His sight!

THE FIFTH LIFE

The Fire and the Garden

The fifth life extends from the time the people of the Fire enter the Fire and the people of the Garden enter the Garden, and continues into unending, limitless eternity.

This is the longest of all lives, the best, most pleasant and most joyous for the people of the Garden, and the worst, hardest, and most hateful and wretched for the people of the Fire.

The Fire

We shall begin by mentioning the Fire and its people, because even believers of *taqwā* will come to it before entering the Garden.

God the Exalted has said: *There is not one of you that shall not come to it. That is a fixed ordinance of your Lord. Then We shall rescue those who had* taqwā, *and leave the unjust therein crouching.* [19:71–2]

O you who believe! Ward off from yourselves and your families a Fire whose fuel is men and stones, over which are set angels, severe, strong, who disobey not God in that which He commands them, but do that which they are commanded. [66:6]

I shall immerse him in Saqar. And what will convey to you what Saqar is? It leaves nothing, spares nothing. [74:26–8]

Therefore have I warned you of the flaming Fire, which only the most wretched shall endure, those who denied and turned away. [92:1–6]

Nay, he will indeed be flung into the Shatterer. And what might convey to you what the Shatterer is? The kindled fire of God, which leaps up over the hearts. It is closed in on them, in outstretched columns. [104:4–9]

We have prepared for the disbelievers a Fire whose tent encloses them. When they ask for help they will be helped with water like molten lead, which burns faces. Evil the drink, and ill the resting-place! [18:29]

Those who disbelieve Our signs, We shall expose them to the Fire. As often as their skins are consumed, We shall exchange them for fresh skins that they may taste the torment. Indeed God is Mighty, Wise. [4:56]

Those who disbelieve, theirs is the fire of Jahannam. They are neither done with and die nor is its torment lightened for them. Therein we punish every disbelieving one. And they cry for help there: 'O Lord! Release us and we will do right, not what we used to do!' Did We not grant you a life long enough for him who reflected to reflect therein? And the warner came to you. [35:37]

And those whose scales are light are those who lose their souls, in Jahannam they abide for evermore. The fire burns their faces, and in it they are livid. Were not My revelations recited to you, and then you used to deny them? They will say: 'Our Lord! Our wretchedness overcame us and we were erring people. Our Lord! Bring us out of it, and if we act thus again, then indeed we shall be unjust.' He will say: 'Begone therein, and speak not unto Me!' [23:103–8]

Indeed the criminals are in Jahannam's torment unceasingly. It is not lightened for them, and in it they despair. We wronged them not, but they it was who were unjust. And they cried: 'O Mālik! Let your Lord make an end of us!' He said: 'You are to remain.' [43:74–7]

Like the verses describing the Fire, the *ḥadīths* are very numerous. We will mention but a few of these, as warnings and reminders.

The Prophet said, may blessings and peace be upon him: 'This fire of yours is one of seventy parts of the fire of Jahannam.' They said: 'O Messenger of God! It is sufficient!' And he told them: 'It has ninety-nine more parts, each as hot as the others'

'The fire of Jahannam was heated for a thousand years until it became red. Then it was heated for a thousand years until it became white. Then it was heated for a thousand years until it became black. It is thus black, and dark.' [*Ḥadīth.*]

'The least tormented of the people of the Fire shall be those who have sandals and laces of fire, and whose heads boil from them as though they were cauldrons. They imagine that none is in more torment than they, yet theirs is the most insignificant torment of them all.' [*Ḥadīth.*]

'Some of them are enveloped by the Fire to their heels, some to their knees, some to their waists, and others to their shoulders.' [*Ḥadīth.*]

'O people! Weep! And if you cannot weep then make as though you were weeping, for the people of the Fire shall weep in Jahannam until their tears run over their faces like streams. Then the tears will stop, blood will flow, and eyes ulcerate, so that if ships were launched therein they would float.' [*Ḥadīth.*]

'Hunger will be cast upon the people of the Fire, until it equals their other torments. They will cry for help, and help will come in the form of *bitter thorn-fruit, which neither nourishes nor releases from hunger.* [88:7] They will cry for help, and will be given food *that they choke on.* They will then remember that in the world they used to relieve choking by drinking; and so they will cry for a drink, and boiling water will be raised to them with iron hooks. When it nears their faces it scorches them, and when it enters their stomachs it lacerates them. They will say: "Call the guards of Jahannam!" And the guards will say: "*Did the Messenger of your Lord not come to you with clear signs?*" "Yes!" they reply. And the guards say: "Call, then, but *the call of the disbelievers can only go astray*!" They will then say: "*O Mālik! Let your Lord make an end of us!" But he will reply: "You shall remain!*"' [43:77] Al-Aʿmash has said: 'Between their calls and Mālik's reply will be a thousand years.' 'They will then say [to each other]: "Call on your Lord, none is better for you than your Lord!" and then: *"Our Lord! Our wretchedness has overcome us, we were a people gone astray. Our Lord! Bring us out of it, and if we repeat [our sin] we will indeed be unjust!"* [23:106–7] *He will answer them: "Begone therein! And speak not to Me!"* [23:108] When this happens, they will lose hope for anything good, and begin to sigh, to lament, and to wail.' [*Ḥadīth*.]

It has been related that in the Fire there are snakes as large as the necks of Bactrian camels, and scorpions as big as mules, the sting of which produces painful fevers for forty autumns. Were a bucket of the rotting drink [*ghassāq*] of Hell to be spilt into the world its stench would affect all the world's inhabitants; and should a drop of the Tree of Zaqqūm[41] be dropped onto the world it would spoil the means of livelihood of all people in the world. And should one of the people of the Fire come out into the world, all the world's inhabitants would die because of his stench and disfigurement.

The Fire's gates are seven, as He has said (Exalted is He!): *It has seven gates, and each gate has an appointed portion of them.* [15:44] It also has seven layers. The first is called *Jahannam*, which is for those among the people of *tawḥīd* who were sinners. The second is called *Saqar*, the third *Laẓā*, the fourth *al-Ḥuṭama*, the fifth *al-Saʿīr*, the sixth *al-Jaḥīm*, and the seventh *al-Hāwiya*. This is the lowermost one, which has neither bottom nor end. These seven layers are filled with agonising torments, hideous tortures, and great humilation, and each layer is worse than the one above it. May God protect us, our parents, our loved ones, and all Muslims, from it, through His grace and generosity!

Know that the people of the Fire are of two kinds: those who are people of *tawḥīd* and enter it because of their sins, and those who are disbelievers [*kāfirūn*], polytheists [*mushrikūn*], and hypocrites [*munāfiqūn*], who outwardly announce their faith but who conceal disbelief within their hearts. The first group will not remain in the Fire forever, for they will leave it through intercession [*shafāʿa*] and God's mercy, but they will nevertheless differ in this: some being taken out before the end of their sentences, and some not. It is said that the last to emerge from it will do so after seven thousand years, which is—according to one opinion—the age of the world. No person of *tawḥīd* will stay in the Fire forever, for those who have as much as an atom's weight of faith will be allowed out, as is stated in sound *ḥadīths*.

People in the second category will remain in the Fire forever: they include the Jews, Christians, Zoroastrians, and others, who are all to remain in the Fire permanently. *Those who disbelieve and die as disbelievers, upon them is the curse of God, and of the angels and men combined. Eternally therein: the torment will not be lightened for them, nor will they be reprieved.* [2:161–6] *God forgives not that a partner be ascribed unto Him, but He forgives all else to whomsoever He will.* [4:48] *Whoso ascribes partners to God, for him God has forbidden the Garden; and his abode shall be the Fire. The unjust shall have no helpers.* [5:72] *The hypocrites shall be in the lowest layer of the Fire.* [4:145]

It has been said that the molar tooth of a disbeliever in the Fire shall be as big as Mount Uḥud, while the thickness of his skin will be forty-two arm lengths, and that they will drag their tongues, which will be one and two leagues long, while people tread on them. God shall enlarge their bodies in the Fire so that their torments may be multiplied and their chastisement made more intense.

When the sinners among the people of *tawḥīd* are brought out from the Fire, until not one of them remains in it, its gates will be locked, and it will close on the disbelievers. *It is indeed closed in on them, in outstretched columns.* [104:8–9] Some of them will be locked in coffins full of fire and left there for eternity, in God's torment, under His abhorrence and wrath, unendingly.

We ask God for wellbeing, to die in Islam, and for protection from the states of the people of the Fire!

The Garden

Know that the verses and *ḥadīths* describing the Garden are very numerous, and we therefore propose to mention only a few, in order to teach and to remind.

And give glad news to those who believe and do good works, that theirs shall be gardens underneath which rivers flow. Each time they are given food of the fruits thereof they say: 'This is what was given us before'—and it is given to them in resemblance. There for them are purified wives. There forever shall they abide. [2:25]

And those who had taqwā *are driven to the Garden in groups, until, when they reach it and its gates are opened, and the guardians say to them: Peace be upon you, you were good, so enter it for evermore! they say: Praise is for God, Who has fulfilled His promise to us and made us inherit the earth, sojourning in the Garden where we will. Fine is the workers' wage! And you see the angels thronging round the Throne, extolling the praise of their Lord; and they are judged aright; and it is said: Praise is for God, Lord of the Worlds!* [39:73–5]

And for those who fear the standing before their Lord there shall be two gardens, until: *So blessed is the Name of your Lord, Possessor of Majesty and Bounty!* [55:45–78]

And the foremost! The foremost! They are those who are brought nigh, in gardens of delight, until: *A multitude of those of old, and a multitude of those of later time.* [56:10–40]

The righteous shall drink of a cup the mixture of which is of camphor, until: *Your endeavour has found acceptance.* [76:5–22]

Enter the Garden, you and your spouses, to be made glad, until: *Therein for you is fruit in plenty whence to eat.* [43:70–3]

Those who had taqwā *will be in a secure place, in gardens and watersprings,* until: *A favour from your Lord: that is the supreme triumph.* [44:51–7]

The likeness of the Garden that people of taqwā *are promised: therein are rivers of water unpolluted, and rivers of milk the flavour of which changes not, and rivers of wine delicious to the drinkers, and rivers of clear honey. There is for them every kind of fruit, and forgiveness from their Lord.* [47:15]

Gardens of Eden, which they enter wearing armlets of gold and pearl, and their raiment therein is silk. And they say: Praise is for God, Who has put grief away from us. Our Lord is Forgiving, Generous. Who, of His grace, has installed us in the mansion of eternity, where toil touches us not, nor can we be affected by weariness. [35:33–5]

And the Garden is brought nigh for those who had taqwā, *not distant. This is what you were promised, for every penitent heedful one, who feared the All-Merciful in secret and came with a contrite heart. Enter it in peace, this is the day of immortality. There they have all that they desire, and We have more.* [50:31–5]

The people of taqwā *will dwell among gardens and rivers, firmly established in the favour of a Mighty King.* [54:54–5]

The Messenger of God, may blessings and peace be upon him, said: 'God the Exalted says: "I have prepared for My virtuous servants that which no eye has seen, no ear has heard, and no human heart imagined." Recite, if you wish: *No soul knows what is kept hidden for them of delightful joy, as reward for what they used to do.'* [32:17]

And he said: 'Two gardens of silver with silver vessels, and two gardens of gold, with golden vessels; and nothing stands between people and the vision of their Lord but the Veil of Glory over His Face, in the Garden of Eden.'

And: 'The Garden comprises one hundred degrees. [The distance] between each two degrees is like the [distance] between Heaven and earth. *Firdaws* is the highest degree, from which spring the four rivers of the Garden. Above it is the Highest Throne. When you petition God, therefore, ask for the *Firdaws*!'

And: 'The area of the Garden which could be surrounded by a whip is better than the world and all that it contains. Should one of the women of the Garden appear to the people of the earth, she would illuminate it entirely, and render it fragrant with musk. The scarf which is upon her head is better than the world and all that it contains.'

And: 'In the Garden there is a tree under the shade of which a rider may travel for a hundred years and still not traverse it. The length of one of your bows in the Garden is better than everything on which the sun has ever risen or set.'

And: 'The believer shall have a tent in the Garden made of a single hollowed pearl, the length of which shall be sixty miles. In each of its corners the believer shall have spouses invisible to the others, and the believer shall visit each of them in turn.'

Abū Hurayra, may God be pleased with him, once asked: 'O Messenger of God! From what was creation created?' And he said: 'From water.'[42] He asked again: 'Of what is the Garden built?' And he replied: 'One brick of gold and one brick of silver; its mortar is fragrant musk, its pebbles are pearls and rubies, its dust is saffron. Those who enter it shall find joy without sorrow, permanence with neither extinction nor death; their clothes shall never wear out, neither shall their youth pass away.'

And: 'The first group to enter the Garden will have faces like the full moon. The second group shall be like the most beautiful scintillating planet in the sky. Each man shall have two wives, each clothed in seventy robes, and the marrow of their legs will be visible through them.'

And: 'The people of the Garden shall enter it beardless, hairless, their eyelids lined with kohl, aged thirty or thirty-three years.'

And he said one day to his Companions: 'Are any of you [willing to] work in earnest for the Garden? For the Garden has no rival. It is, by the Lord of the Kaʿba, a scintillating light, a swaying, fragrant plant, a lofty palace, a flowing river, a multitude of ripe fruits, a comely wife, and many garments, in a perpetual abode of life and vigour, in a lofty house of soundness and splendour.' They said: 'We are the ones who shall work for it in earnest, O Messenger of God!' And he said: 'Say: "If God the Exalted so wills!"'

And he said likewise: 'The palm trees of the Garden shall have trunks of green emeralds, palm roots of red gold, and its palms shall be clothes for the people of the Garden, from which their garments and robes are made. Its fruits are the size of jugs and pails, whiter then milk, sweeter than honey, softer than butter, devoid of stones.'

And: 'The people of the Garden eat and drink, and neither spit, urinate, pass excrement nor blow their noses.' They asked: 'What about the food?' and he replied: 'Belching, and perspiration like sprinkled musk.[43] They are inspired to extol, hallow and praise God.' And in another version of this *ḥadīth* the following is added: 'And glorify, just as they have been inspired to breathe.'

And he has said, may blessings and peace be upon him: 'Men among the people of the Garden will each be given the strength of a hundred in eating, drinking, sexual intercourse, and desire.'

And: 'A herald shall announce: "O people of the Garden! It is time for you to be healthy and never fall ill. It is time for you to live and never die. It is time for you to be young and never grow old. And it is time for you to be happy and never be miserable.' This is His saying, Exalted is He!: *And they are called: This is the Garden, you have inherited it because of that which you used to do*. [7:43]

And he was asked: 'What is al-Kawthar?' He replied: 'A river in the Garden given to me by God, whiter than milk, sweeter than honey, on which are birds with necks like the necks of camels.' And ʿUmar said: 'Those are indeed in pleasure.' He said: 'Those who eat them are in even greater pleasure.'

And he said: 'I met Abraham, upon whom be peace, on the night of the *Isrā'*, and he said: "O Muḥammad! Give my greetings to your *Umma*, and inform them that the Garden has fragrant soil, sweet water, and is made of plains the planting of which is *Subḥān Allāh, al-ḥamdu li'Llāh, Lā ilāha illa'Llāh, wa'Llāhu akbar*.'[44]

And: 'In the Garden there are rooms the outside of which can be seen from within, and the inside from without.' A bedouin got up and said: 'For whom shall they be, O Messenger of God?' and he replied: 'For those who speak with goodness, feed [the people], fast regularly, and pray by night while others sleep.'

And: 'God will address the people of the Garden, saying: "O people of the Garden!" "At your service, O Lord!" they will say, "At your pleasure! All goodness is in Your hands."

"Are you content?" he asks them, and they reply: "How may we not be content, O Lord, when You have given us what no creature of Yours has ever been given?" And He says: "Shall I then give you that which is better still?" and they ask him: "O Lord! What could be better still?" "I shall grant you My good pleasure [*riḍwān*]," He says, "and shall never be wrathful against you again."'

It has been been reported that the poor among the Muslims will enter the Garden half a day before the rich (and this is five hundred years), that the rivers of the Garden flow on its surface without furrows, that the height [of people there] will be sixty cubits (the height of their forefather Adam), that the least among them shall receive ten times as much as the [whole] world, has a thousand servants, seventy-two *ḥūrīs* for wives, and that it will take him a thousand years to see all the gifts and honour that God has prepared for him, that every tree-trunk in the Garden is made of gold, that the gates of the Garden are eight, and that its degrees are as many as the number of verses in the Noble Qur'ān. May God make us among its people, through His Grace and Generosity. Āmīn!

AFTERWORD

THE VISION OF GOD, AND HIS OVERWHELMING MERCY

We now provide an afterword to this life, and thereby, God willing, conclude the whole book.

The believers will see their Lord (Blessed and Exalted is He!) in the Garden. *For those who do good is the best reward, and still more.* [10:26]

This verse has been given the commentary that 'the best reward' refers to the Garden, while 'still more' refers to the vision of God, the High and Majestic. *That day faces will be resplendent, looking towards their Lord.* [75:22–3]

The Messenger of God, may blessings and peace be upon him, said: 'After the people of the Garden have entered the Garden, He Who is Blessed and Exalted shall ask: "Do you wish Me to give you anything more?" And they will reply: "Have You not brightened our faces? Have You not made us enter the Garden and saved us from the Fire?" He will then remove the veil, and nothing they were ever given will have been dearer to them than the vision of their Lord, the High, the Majestic.' And in another version he recited: *'For those who do good is the best reward, and still more.'*

Jābir ibn ʿAbdallāh, may God be pleased with him, said: 'We were once with the Messenger of God, may blessings and peace be upon him, when he looked at the full moon, and then said: "You will see your Lord with your eyes as you see this moon. You will not be hindered from seeing Him. Therefore if you can manage to pray before sunrise and before sunset, do so!" Then he recited: *Extol the praises of your Lord before sunrise and before sunset.'* [20:130] The two prayers meant here are the morning [*fajr*] and afternoon [*ʿaṣr*] prayers.

Abū Razīn al-ʿUqaylī asked: 'O Messenger of God! Will

we all see God, without obstruction, on the Day of Rising?' He said: 'Yes.' He then asked: 'What is the sign of that in His creation?' and the Prophet replied: 'O Abū Razīn! Do you not all see the moon, without obstruction, on the night when it is full?' He said: 'Indeed we do.' 'God is greater,' he told him, 'and that is but a creature of God's creation, Who is High and Majestic.'

And the Prophet said, may blessings and peace be upon him: 'The people of the Garden when they enter it will be situated according to the merits of their deeds. Then they will be allowed to visit their Lord for a time equivalent to that of Friday in the world. His Throne will come down to them, and He will manifest himself before them in a meadow of the Garden. A dais of light will be erected for them, and a dais of pearl, a dais of ruby, and a dais of chrysolite, a dais of gold, and a dais of silver; and the lowest of them—and none of them is low—will sit on dunes of musk and camphor, and will not feel that those on chairs are better seated.'

Abū Hurayra said: 'O Messenger of God! Shall we see our Lord?' He replied: 'Yes! Do you doubt your seeing the sun and the moon?' Abū Hurayra said: 'No!' And he said: 'Similarly you will not doubt seeing your Lord. None will remain in that gathering but that God will converse with him, to the extent that He will say to each man: "O so-and-so, son of so-and-so! Do you remember the day you said such-and-such a thing?" And He will remind him of some shortcoming of his in the world, and the man will say: "Did You not forgive?" Then He will reply: "Indeed, it is through the broadness of My forgiveness that you have reached this degree." And as they thus converse a cloud will come over them, and shall rain on them a perfume the scent of which they had never experienced before. And our Lord will say: "Come to the honour I have prepared for you; take whatever you wish!" They will go to a market surrounded by angels the like of which no eye has ever seen, no ear ever heard, and no heart ever imagined. There they will take whatever they desire, for there will be neither selling nor buying, and in that market the people of the Garden shall meet one other. A man of high rank may meet someone of lower rank—and none of them are low—and he will be amazed by the clothes he will see him wearing. Their conversation will not end before he sees even better ones on him, for there should be no sadness there. Then we will return home to be met by our spouses who will greet and welcome us, and declare that we have returned with even more beauty than when we had left them, and we will reply: "We have met our Lord the Compeller. It is our right to return with what we have returned with".'

The greatest, highest, most noble and perfect felicity is to see the Noble Face of God in the abode of honour and of bliss. May God grant us this, purely through His Grace, Generosity, and Munificence, and grant it also to our parents, our loved ones, and all Muslims, by His Mercy; for He is the Most Merciful!

My Mercy embraces all things. [7:156] *Inform My slaves that I am indeed the Forgiving, the Merciful.* [15:49] *Say: Peace be upon you! Your Lord has prescribed mercy upon Himself, that whoever of you does evil and repents afterward of that, and does right, God is Forgiving, Merciful.* [6:54] *Say: O My servants, who have been prodigal with their own selves! Despair not of God's Mercy! God forgives all sins. He is the Forgiving, the Merciful.* [39:53] *Whoso does evil or wrongs his own soul, then seeks God's forgiveness, will find God to be Forgiving, Merciful.* [4:110]

The Messenger of God, may blessings and peace be upon him, said: 'God has a hundred mercies, one of which He has sent down to be divided between humans, jinn, birds, cattle, and insects, and by which they have compassion and mercy towards each other. And He has saved ninety-nine mercies, with which He will be merciful to His slaves on the Day of Rising.'

It has been related that on the Day of Rising, God will cause this inscription to appear from beneath the Throne: 'My Mercy has outstripped My wrath, and I am the Most

Merciful of the Merciful.' And then as many as the people of the Garden will be let out of the Fire.

And the Prophet said, may blessings and peace be upon him: 'God has more compassion for His believing slave than a mother has for her child.'

And: 'God will have such forgiveness that [even] Iblīs will hope to be reached by it.' But Iblīs, may God curse him, cannot be included under any circumstance in God's forgiveness, for he is among those who have despaired and lost hope in God's forgiveness and mercy, and he is the leader of the polytheists. *God forgives not that a partner should be ascribed to Him, but He forgives all else to whomsoever He will.* [4:48]

And he said, may blessings and peace be upon him: 'God will forbid the Fire to take anyone who affirms that there is no god but God and that Muḥammad is the Messenger of God.'

And: 'A herald shall call from underneath the Throne on the Day of Rising: "O Nation of Muḥammad! Whatever you owe Me I release you from, and whatever you owe each other, release each other from it! Then enter the Garden through My mercy.'

This ends all that we wished to include in this treatise, which, God willing, is a blessed one. All *baraka* is from God. Grace and goodness are in God's hand. The whole matter is God's. There is neither ability nor strength save by God the High, the Tremendous. God is Sufficient for us, and He is the best of guardians.

O Lord! Accept our deeds, for You are the Hearer, the Knower! Relent towards us, for You are the Relenter, the Merciful! *Our Lord! Cause not our hearts to stray after You have guided us, and bestow upon us mercy from Your Presence. You, only You, are the Bestower.* [3:8] *Flood us with patience, and take us to You as Muslims!* [7:126]

May God bless our master Muḥammad, His slave and His Messenger, trustworthy in the revelation, together with his pure, fragrant family, and his well-guided and well-guiding

Companions, and those who excel in following them until the Day of Reckoning, and us along with them, through Your Mercy, O Most Merciful of the Merciful!

The treatise stands concluded, God be thanked, through His assistance and gracious bestowal of success. Its dictation ended on the morning of Sunday the twenty-ninth of Shaʿbān in the year 1110 of the *Hijra*, may the best of blessings and most fragrant peace be on the *Muhājir*.

Praise and thanks are for God,
the Lord of the Worlds

NOTES

1 In view of some well-known contemporary concerns, we should affirm that the contents of this book are equally applicable to both sexes, and that the masculine form of the pronoun is inclusive of the feminine. For confirmation of this see, for instance, Imām Suyūṭī's *Tuḥfat al-julasā'*.

2 It is important to remember throughout this book that 'happy' (*saʿīd*) and 'wretched' (*shaqī*) refer principally to man's destiny in the after-death state.

3 The 'people of the Right' (*aṣḥāb al-yamīn*) are those destined for salvation, while the 'people of the Left' (*aṣḥāb al-shimāl*) are destined for damnation.

The expression 'the two fistfuls' is a reference to the famous *ḥadīth* in which a dying man once said, 'I heard God's Messenger (upon him be blessings and peace) say: 'God the Blessed and Exalted took a fistful with His right hand, and said: "This is for this [the Garden], and I do not mind," and took another fistful with His left hand, and said: "This is for this [the Fire], and I do not mind".' And I do not know in which of the two fistfuls I lie.' (Ibn Ḥanbal, V, 68.)

4 The following verse runs: *Or lest you should say: It is only that our fathers ascribed partners to God of old, and we were [their] seed after them. Wilt Thou destroy us on account of that which those who follow falsehood did?*

5 For the full text of this *ḥadīth*, narrated by Imām Muslim, see Robson's translation of the *Mishkāt al-Maṣābīḥ*, I, 23.

6 The Torah (*tawrāh*): the ancient scripture revealed by God to Moses.

7 I.e. what they wear is all they have.

8 Cited in *Ṭahārat al-Qulūb* by Shaykh ʿAbd al-ʿAzīz al-Dīrīnī. [Author's note.]

9 Ghazālī, *Iḥyā' ʿUlūm al-Dīn* (Beirut, 1406), III, 45–6.

10 *Ḥadīth* related by Imām Muslim, Imāra, 133.

11 As these passages affirm, the age of forty is the pivot, the turning point, after which one's life in general works out the consequences of how one's soul was shaped during one's youth. In this connection it is interesting to recall the remark of Oscar Wilde, that 'by the age of forty, every man has the face that he deserves.'

12 Nothing could be more striking than the contrast between the upright dignity of an elderly Muslim, surrounded by respectful

family and friends, and the unseemly descent into churlishness and hopeless desire so common among ageing unbelievers.

13 See the translation by Muhammad Abul Quasem, *Al-Ghazali on Islamic Guidance*, p. 56.

14 Ibid., 43.

15 This *ḥadīth*, which is narrated by Imām Bukhārī, expounds an attitude which is forgotten by some Muslims of our generation, who believe that the world is of some value in its own right. How often one hears the *ḥadīth*: 'work for the *dunyā* as though you were to live forever, and work for the *ākhira* as though you were to die tomorrow,' cited by those who are partial to large cars and swelling bank accounts, forgetting the true, traditional interpretation of the *ḥadīth*, which is 'work for the *dunyā* without haste, and for the *ākhira* with great urgency'. The matter was summed up by our master Ḥātim al-Aṣamm, who declared: 'Work for your *dunyā* in accordance with the length of your stay therein. Work for your *ākhira* in accordance with the length of your stay therein. Work for the Fire in accordance with your ability to endure it. And work for God in accordance with your need for Him.'

16 In Arabic: *Allāhumma innā nas'aluka bi-nūri wajhika'l-karīm, wabi-ḥaqqika ᶜalayk, ḥusn al-khātima ᶜinda al-mamāt, lanā wali-aḥbābinā wali'l-muslimīna yā arḥam ar-rāḥimīn. "Rabbanā lā tuzigh qulūbanā baᶜda idh hadaytanā wahab lanā min ladunka raḥma, innaka anta'l-Wahhāb." "Rabbanā afrigh ᶜalaynā ṣabran watawaffanā muslimīn".*

17 As stated in a famous *ḥadīth*: 'Death is the gift to the believer.' (Related by al-Ḥākim al-Nīsābūrī.)

18 A serious skin disease.

19 This account, if it is in fact authentic, applies to whoever is wished goodness by God, and is in a state of felicity, and grows up in rectitude, righteousness and Islam, and is blessed with success in doing good works, and for whom sins and evildoing are made hateful in his prolonged life. And God knows best. [Note by Shaykh Ḥasanayn Makhlūf.]

20 *Innā li'Llāhi wa'innā ilayhi rājiᶜūn.*

21 ᶜIllīyīn: the book where the acts of the righteous are recorded. See Qur'ān, 83:18–21.

22 *Allāhumma 'jᶜal kitābahu fī ᶜillīyīn, wa'ktubhu ᶜindaka min al-muḥsinīn, wa'khlufhu fī ahlihi fi'l-ghābirīn, wa'ghfir lanā wa-lahu yā rabb al-ᶜālamīn.*

23 For more on this *ḥadīth* see Imām Ghazālī, *The Remembrance of Death and the Afterlife*, p. 119.

24 Before they rot away [Note by Shaykh Ḥasanayn Makhlūf].

25 *Bismillāh, wa-ᶜalā millat Rasūlillāh.*

26 Saʿd ibn Muʿādh was a Medinan nobleman who died of wounds received at the Battle of al-Khandaq.

27 In Arabic: *as-salāmu ʿalaykum dāra qawmin mu'minīn. Ghadan mu'ajjalūn, wa-atākum mā tūʿadūn, wa-innā in shā' Allāhu bikum lāḥiqūn. Antum lanā salafun wa-naḥnu lakum tabaʿ. Nas'alu 'Llāha lanā wa-lakumu 'l-ʿāfiya. Allāhumma 'ghfir lanā wa-lahum.*

28 Jūj and Ma'jūj. Two large communities which will appear before the end of time, and wreak havoc in the earth. According to many authors, they will appear from Central Asia.

29 ʿUkāẓ: a market town near Makka famed for the quality of its leather.

30 The 'Horn' (*al-ṣūr*) is an immense trumpet made of light, whose great size is known only to God the Exalted.

31 Imām al-Ḥaddād here suggests that we read the following verses as well (18:48–54), which he does not quote, assuming, probably, that we know them by heart.

32 'Syria' here means all the lands between Iraq and the eastern borders of Sinai.

33 'Usury' here refers to *ribā*, which includes any money gained or paid as interest.

34 A 'mile' (*mīl*) in Arabic is usually defined as extending as far as one's vision reaches.

35 See Ibn Ḥanbal, *Musnad*, III, 75: The Messenger of God, upon whom be blessings and peace, said: 'By Him in Whose hand lies my soul, it shall be shortened for the believer until it becomes briefer for him than the obligatory prayer which he used to perform in the world.'

36 Rabīʿa and Muḍar: two Arabian tribes possessed of vast numbers of sheep.

37 *Iḥyā' ʿUlūm al-Dīn*, book 40. An English translation exists; see the Bibliography.

38 *al-Durrat al-Fākhira fī Kashf ʿUlūm al-Ākhira*, printed many times. There is an English translation available.

39 *al-Tadhkira fī Aḥwāl al-Mawtā wa-Umūr al-Ākhira*. See Bibliography.

40 [I] *Sharḥ al-ṣudūr bi-sharḥ ḥāl al-mawtā wa'l-qubūr*. [II] *al-Budūr al-Sāfira fī aḥwāl al-Ākhira*. Mention might also be made of his *Bushrā al-ka'īb bi-liqā' al-Ḥabīb*, his *Tuḥfat al-julasā' bi-ru'yat Allāh li'l-nisā'*, and his *al-Durar al-ḥisān fi'l-baʿth wa-naʿīm al-jinān*.

41 Zaqqūm: *A tree that grows from the bottom of hell, whose crop is like the heads of devils. They must eat thereof, and fill their bellies from it.* (37:64–6; see also 44:43–6.)

42 Qur'ān 21:30: *And from water did We create every living thing.*

43 I.e., instead of waste matter being disposed of in the usual fashion, it

will leave the body in the form of belching and perspiration.

44 Qur'ānic formulas regularly repeated by Muslims, meaning 'Sublime is God, praise is for God, there is no deity but God, and God is most great'.

GLOSSARY OF ARABIC TERMS

Aʿrāf. Boundary area, or limbo, between the Fire and the Garden, occupied by those who are deserving of neither.

ʿArafāt. Plain near Makka which witnesses the culminating event of the Ḥajj.

Barzakh. The 'intermediate world': which includes the life in the grave between death and resurrection.

Dajjāl. The Antichrist.

Dunyā. This world, as opposed to the *ākhira*, which signifies the other world, the world-to-come.

Ḥawḍ. The vast lake to which the believers shall come on the Day of Judgement.

ʿIllīyyīn. A book in which the actions of the righteous are recorded.

Iqāma. The short *adhān* made just before the prayer begins.

Isrā'. The 'night journey' of the Prophet, upon whom be blessings and peace, from Makka to Jerusalem.

Jahannam. Hellfire.

Miʿrāj. The ascension of the Prophet, upon whom be blessings and peace, through the heavens to the Presence of God.

Qibla. The direction of the Sacred House in Makka.

Saqar. A place in Hell.

Ṣirāṭ. The bridge stretched over Hell on the Day of Judgement.

Sunna. The pattern of life of the Blessed Prophet, which comprises the norm and example for his followers.

Sūrat al-Ikhlāṣ. Sura 112 of the Qur'ān.

Talbiya. The pilgrims on their way to the House say: "*Labbayk Allahumma Labbayk*" (Here I am O God! At Your service!). This is *talbiya*.

Taqwā. Awareness of God, and hence careful observance of His law.

Tashahhud. 'Bearing witness': the devotional phrases said towards the end of the *ṣalāt* prayer.

Tawḥīd. Belief in God's Oneness and Uniqueness.

Umma. The 'nation', or world-community, of Islam.

INDEX OF PROPER NAMES

All dates conform to the Muslim calendar

ʿAbd al-Wahhāb al-Shaʿrānī (d.973). Great jurist and devotional writer of Cairo.

ʿAbdallāh ibn ʿAlī (al-ʿAydarūs) (d. 1131). Ḥaḍramī scholar who was a friend of Imām al-Ḥaddād.

ʿAbdallāh ibn Abī Bakr al-ʿAydarūs Bā-ʿAlawī (d.865). Known as al-ʿAydarūs al-Akbar. The grandson of Imām ʿAbd al-Raḥmān al-Saqqāf, he was one of the best-known religious leaders ever produced by South Arabia.

Abū Hurayra (d.58). Famous Companion and narrator of *ḥadīths*.

Abū Razīn al-ʿUqaylī. Companion.

al-Aʿmash (d.147). A famous early scholar of the Qur'ān, who dwelt at Kūfa.

Anas ibn Mālik (d.91). A Companion who narrated a large number of *ḥadīth*.

al-Faqīh al-Muqaddam. This is Muḥammad ibn ʿAlī (d.653), regarded as one of the greatest luminaries of the ʿAlawī family of Ḥaḍramawt.

al-Ghazālī (d.505). Author of the best-known works on Islamic jurisprudence, Sufism and theology, and refuter of the Arab philosophers and the Ismāʿīlīs. These multifarious services earned him the title of Ḥujjat al-Islām: the 'Proof of Islam', from a grateful Islamic world.

Iblīs. The devil, may God curse him.

Isrāfīl. The angel whose task it is to blow the Trumpet for Judgement Day.

Jābir ibn ʿAbdallāh (d.68). A Companion who related a number of important *ḥadīths*.

Jaʿfar al-Ṣādiq (d.148). A Madīnan expert on Islamic law, later regarded by the Shīʿa as one of their Imāms.

al-Khaṭīb ibn Nubāta (d.374). A Syrian preacher famous for his sermons in elaborate rhyming prose, delivered at the court of the sultan of Aleppo.

al-Ma'mūn (d.218). ʿAbbāsid caliph.

Mālik. The angel who supervises Hell.

Maʿrūf al-Karkhī (d.200). An important early Sufi who taught *ḥadīth* to Aḥmad ibn Ḥanbal.

Mīkā'īl. The angel who distributes wealth and sustenance.

Muʿādh ibn Jabal (d.18). Companion and *ḥadīth* narrator.

Mūsā al-Kāẓim (d. 183). Well-known scholar of Medina.

al-Nawawī (d.676). Shāfiʿī, Ashʿarī and Sufi scholar of Damascus, collector of the famous *Forty Ḥadīth*.

al-Qurṭubī, Shams al-Dīn (d.671). One of the last outstanding Muslim scholars to appear in al-Andalus before its destruction by European savagery. He authored a famous *Tafsīr*, and was widely respected for his ascetic lifestyle.

Saʿd ibn Muʿādh (d. 5). A Companion praised by the Prophet, upon whom be blessings and peace, for his heroism at the Battle of al-Khandaq, which led to his martyrdom.

al-Shāfiʿī (d.204). Founder of the Shāfiʿī school, one of the four orthodox schools of Islamic Law. The ʿAlawī *sayyids*, including Imām al-Ḥaddād himself, are followers of his school.

ʿUmar ibn ʿAbd al-ʿAzīz (d. 101). Devout caliph whose reign saw concerted attempts to rectify injustices and violations of the *Sharīʿa*.

ʿUthmān ibn ʿAffān (d.35). The third 'Rightly-guided Caliph,' during whose reign numerous conquests took place.

APPENDIX

It may be of interest to readers if we provide a list of the best-known Arabic texts which deal with the subject of the Judgement, Heaven and Hell.

1 al-Ḥārith al-Muḥāsibī (d.243) of Baghdad. *Al-Tawahhum*. (*The Imagining*.) This is a remarkable description of the life-to-come, in which the reader is asked to imagine that he is physically present on a visit beyond the grave. The book, which was published in Cairo by A.J. Arberry in 1937, has recently been translated into French.

2 Imām Abū Ḥāmid al-Ghazālī (d.505) of Nisabur. *Al-Durra al-Fākhira*. (*The Precious Pearl*.) Contains a large number of picturesque hadiths of doubtful provenance. Most ulema believe it not to have been written by Imām al-Ghazālī at all. An English translation exists.

3 Imām Abū Ḥāmid al-Ghazālī. *Dhikr al-Mawt wa-mā Baʿdahu*. (*Remembering Death and what follows it*.) This is in fact the last section of his famous *Iḥyāʾ ʿUlūm al-Dīn*. As well as describing the states of the next world, and providing an exquisite chapter on the death of the Messenger (may blessings and peace be upon him), it contains what is probably the best examination ever written of the problem of forgetfulness (*ghafla*) of death and the Hereafter. Like all of the *Iḥyāʾ*, it has always been at the centre of Muslim intellectual and devotional life; as Imām al-Nawawī remarked: 'Were all the books of Islam to be lost, except only the *Iḥyāʾ*, it would compensate for all that had been lost.' An English translation of this section is now available.

4 Ibn Rajab al-Ḥanbalī (d.795) of Baghdad. *Ahwāl al-Qubūr*. (*Terrors of the Graves*.) A useful collection of *ḥadīths* and other material about the *Barzakh*.

5 Ibn Qayyim al-Jawziyya (d.751) of Damascus. *al-Rūḥ*. (*The Spirit*.) A long study of the human spirit, written by one of the greatest of all Islamic scholars. Much material is borrowed from Ghazālī, but there is a fascinating and unique section on the 'Day of the Covenant', when all souls were taken out of the loins of Adam, upon whom be peace, and declared their *tawḥīd*. A brief but useful extract exists in English.

6 ʿAbd al-Raḥīm al-Qāḍī, *Daqāʾiq al-Akhbār*. (*The Precise Reports*.) Popular but rather inauthentic collection of hadiths and stories.

7 Shams al-Dīn al-Qurṭubī (d.671) of Cordova. *Al-Tadhkira*. (*The Memorial*.) Written by the author of the famous *Tafsīr*, this is the longest of all popular books on the subject. As a result it is often read in an abridged version usually ascribed to Imām al-Shaʿrānī (d.973). Includes much material on Imām Mahdī and the Dajjāl.

8 Imām Jalāl al-Dīn al-Suyūṭī (d.911). *Sharḥ al-Sudūr*. (*Opening of Hearts*.) A collection of *ḥadīths* and other material about life in the grave.

9 Imām ʿAbdallāh al-Ḥaddād (d.1132) of Tarīm. *Sabīl al-Iddikār*. (*The Lives of Man*.)

Although all the above can be read with profit, it is hardly necessary to read them all. We would say that it is enough for most Muslims to read the *Remembrance of Death* by Imām Ghazālī, and the *Lives of Man* by Imām al-Ḥaddād.

WORKS CITED

Ghazālī, Abū Ḥāmid al-. *Iḥyā' ʿulūm al-dīn*. Beirut, 1406.

—— *The Remembrance of Death and the Afterlife* (tr. T J Winter). Cambridge, 1989 CE.

—— *al-Durra al-Fākhira fi kashf ʿulūm al-ākhira*. Cairo, 1356. (Translated by Jane Smith as *The Precious Pearl*, Missoula, 1979 CE.)

—— *Bidāyat al-hidāya*. Cairo, 1321. (Tr. Muhammad Abul Quasem, as *Al-Ghazali on Islamic Guidance* (Kuala Lumpur, 1979 CE).)

Ḥaddād, ʿAbdallāh ibn ʿAlawī, al-. *Sabīl al-iddikār wa'l-iʿtibār bimā yamurru bi'l-insān wa-yanqaḍī lahu min al-aʿmār*. Cairo, 1392, and reprints.

Ibn Ḥanbal, Aḥmad. *al-Musnad*. Cairo, 1313.

Ibn Qayyim al-Jawziyya, *Kitāb al-Rūḥ*. Hyderabad 1357. (Extract translated as *The Soul's Journey after Death*, by Aisha Bewley (London, 1987 CE).)

Ibn Rajab al-Ḥanbalī, *Ahwāl al-qubūr wa-aḥwāl ahlihā ilā al-nushūr*. Cairo, 1376.

Muḥāsibī, al-Ḥārith al-. *Kitāb al-Tawahhum*. Cairo, 1937 CE. (French translation by André Roman as *Une vision humaine des fins dernières* (Paris 1978 CE).)

al-Qāḍī, ʿAbd al-Raḥīm. *Daqā'iq al-akhbār fi dhikr al-janna wa'l-nār*. Cairo, 1345. (Translated by A'isha al-Tarjumana as The Islamic *Book of the Dead*, (Norwich, 1977 CE).)

Qurṭubī, Shams al-Dīn, al-. *al-Tadhkira fi aḥwāl al-mawtā wa-umūr al-ākhira*. Cairo, 1352.

Shaʿrānī, ʿAbd al-Wahhāb, al-. *Mukhtaṣar tadhkirat al-Qurṭubī*. Cairo 1326.

Suyūṭī, Jalāl al-Dīn, al-. *al-Budūr al-Sāfira fi aḥwāl al-Ākhira*, Cairo, n.d.

—— *Bushrā al-ka'īb biliqā' al-Ḥabīb*. Cairo, 1359.

—— *Sharḥ al-ṣudūr bisharḥ ḥāl al-mawtā wa'l- qubūr*. Cairo, 1359.

—— *Tuḥfat al-julasā' bi-ru'yat Allāh li'l-nisā'*. Beirut, 1404.

—— *al-Durar al-ḥisān fi'l-baʿth wa-naʿīm al-jinān*. Cairo, 1359.

Tabrīzī, tr. Robson. *Mishkāt al-Maṣābīḥ*, Lahore, 1970 CE.

GENERAL INDEX